GATHER ME

GATHER ME

A MEMOIR IN PRAISE OF

THE BOOKS THAT SAVED ME

Glory Edim

BALLANTINE BOOKS

New York

Published in the United States by Ballantine Books, an imprint of Random House, a division of Penguin Random House LLC, New York.

BALLANTINE BOOKS & colophon are registered trademarks of Penguin Random House LLC.

Hardback ISBN 978-0-525-61979-6
Ebook ISBN 978-0-525-61980-2

Printed in the United States of America on acid-free paper

randomhousebooks.com

9 8 7 6 5 4 3 2 1

First Edition

Book design by Debbie Glasserman

This book is dedicated to my son, Zikomo

My love for you is unconditional.

May you always know the power of your voice and story.

She is a friend of my mind. She gather me, man. The pieces I am, she gather them and give them back to me in all the right order. It's good, you know, when you got a woman who is a friend of your mind.

—TONI MORRISON, *Beloved*

PROLOGUE

Davis, Giovanni, West, Brooks, Butler, Lorde, hooks, Adichie, Shange, Kincaid, Hurston, Naylor, Angelou, Bambara, Walker, Hansberry, Morrison, Smith, Sanchez.

At the lowest points in my life, the most isolated and difficult times, when I was sad, when I was confused, or frozen, or drifting, or desperate, I reached for a book.

When I was joyful, successful, well nourished, and content, I reached for a book.

When the people I depended on disappeared or turned their backs, when I was handed what felt like too much to bear, when I was trying to do right by those I loved, when I was desperately trying to block out the raised voices in the room next to mine, or waiting for an answer that never came, when I needed a word to break the silence that surrounded me, I reached for a book.

And when I moved to Brooklyn, ready to start my life fresh, to shake off some hard years and finally figure out who I really was, I reached for a book.

Books have been my ladder, my stepping-stones, my therapist, my teacher, my medicine, my parents, my religion, my lover, my fool, my instructional manual for life. Words, sentences, pages, and chapters have echoed my loneliness, reflected my joy, guided me to the shadowy corners of my heart and soul that needed to be coaxed into the light, given me strength, helped me grow and change. Books taught me to bloom.

Books gave me my direction. My career. My community. My chosen family. My purpose.

STRANGELY ENOUGH, THOUGH, THE WELL-READ BLACK GIRL Book Club started not with a book but with a T-shirt.

I have written about this before, but let me embroider upon it a bit now, tell the parts that I have left out. My partner at the time and I, like so many young romances, had a tempestuous beginning. We met in college, then broke up, and then got back together. We were petty and then profound. We argued and made up. We split and broke and then mended things. We'd fling apart like petals in the wind, and a week or two later, be pulled back into each other's orbit. Sometimes it was my decision, sometimes it was his, sometimes we mutually agreed, sometimes it felt like something beyond our control.

We were in one of our more extended breaks when he gave me the shirt. It was my thirty-second birthday. I was living in a dusty sublet in Brooklyn that I'd found in a hurry after our breakup—sharing it with two roommates who felt like strangers—and I was feeling very sorry for myself. I had come to Brooklyn eight years before to find community, to stretch my wings, to connect with a big, rich, new world. Instead, I felt like an outsider, a wallflower, a fraud. Everyone around me seemed to fit in in a way that I didn't, and as hard as I tried, I just couldn't manage to get their attention. They seemed either actively uninterested in me or simply too busy to bother. I loved to talk, but I had no one to talk to. I felt most at ease in a community, but I was isolated and alone. I had left my family behind in D.C., and I was expecting a miserable, lonely birthday.

Instead, a gift was delivered. A little package from my ex, with a stack of my favorite magazines on top and a chocolate-brown T-shirt on the bottom. The shirt said WELL-READ BLACK GIRL in large letters and ERUDITA PUELLA AFRICAE, 12/22 (my birthdate) in smaller ones. And in the middle, there was an emblem—a crest of sorts—consisting of an open book, a crown, and a laurel wreath. This was encircled by the names of all my favorite authors: DAVIS, GIOVANNI, WEST, BROOKS, BUTLER, LORDE, HOOKS, ADICHIE, SHANGE, KINCAID, HURSTON, NAYLOR, ANGELOU, BAMBARA, WALKER, HANSBERRY, MORRISON, SMITH, SANCHEZ. (Chant those names out loud and you have something that feels as powerful as any prayer.)

The shirt was magic. But probably not in the way you are thinking. Though my ex and I did reunite soon after, the shirt didn't really fix anything between us. It didn't cast a spell that created a traditional happily ever after. We continued our on-again, off-again relationship for some years more. We continued to fight and make up. We continued our push and pull. We had a child together—our beloved son, Zikomo (who, it seems to me now, was the true reason we were initially brought together). We tried to make it work. Until it simply didn't anymore.

This is a love story. But it is not *that* kind of love story.

Reader, I kept the shirt, but not the man.

THE FIRST YEAR AFTER I RECEIVED THE SHIRT, I WORE IT often, and every time I slipped it onto my skin, it worked its magic. Suddenly people—these same New Yorkers who had been gazing straight past me for what felt like months— stopped and smiled and talked to me. They would glance over at me on the subway, or in a line at the bodega, and ask where I got the T-shirt. What it meant.

And then, the best thing of all started to happen; people started talking to me about books. Their favorite authors, their favorite stories. They'd ask who I loved, what I recommended. They'd quote lines of poetry and remember a fairy tale their mom had read to them when they were young. They talked about their beloved high school teachers or lit professors in college. They would connect with me in the most enthusiastic and joyful way. Suddenly, I understood how I would find my people, my community, how I could build fellowship and make those connections I'd been longing for.

I would create a book club. The Well-Read Black Girl Book Club.

And books would save me again.

I HAVE A PRAYER THAT I SAY TO MYSELF ON AN ALMOST daily basis. *God, help me suspend my disbelief.*

Even now, all these years later, I sometimes think, *What is happening? How did I get this lucky? How am I doing this? How can this be my life?*

This grace was not something I planned on or anticipated.

For much of my childhood and young adulthood, I struggled. I struggled with loss, and I struggled with fear, and I struggled with the fact that my family needed me. Not just in the usual way but as a primary caretaker and a breadwinner as well. I had been asked to punch above my weight since I was thirteen years old, and we were essentially transient by the time I was eighteen.

Growing up, I learned to keep secrets. I learned to clutch the hard, shadowy, shameful things about my family close to my chest, where I thought no one could ever see them, where they slowly dripped and leaked and corroded my heart with their poison.

But Well-Read Black Girl taught me to open my hands and loosen my tongue. To say those secrets out loud. It taught me to reframe my childhood. To acknowledge the pain, but also to remember the other, safer world I built for myself out of paper and ink. The world that allowed me to survive. To ask for help when I needed it the most: as a daughter, sister, mother, and friend. My faithful community of dedicated readers and exceptional writers have served as a beacon of light, providing me with a sanctuary where I can show up as myself, reflect, and heal.

When you're in a situation where your household is uncertain or traumatic, when you are lonely and stuck, you learn the hard way that things could certainly always get worse. Because they often do. But sometimes, amid the chaos, there can be a word, or a sentence, or an entire page that creates a flicker of warmth, of light—the smallest literary flame that can illuminate a new and more hopeful path. It can show you that there are entire universes to be explored, that one morning you might wake up somewhere completely new. Somewhere safer, stronger, more forgiving. A place filled with grace and joy. Through community, I have found refuge, understanding, and the gentle reassurance that I am never alone.

The T-shirt, the books, the authors, the club, the community: Those things are now my bright and roaring fire, my blessed and beautiful universe.

Books and Well-Read Black Girl finally made me feel like I belonged. Not just in the city—though that was true, too—but in a bigger way. I had a home. A network. A support system. An extended, chosen family. And I had a purpose. The club, my sisters who joined me, the books we read, the authors who spoke, the stories we absorbed—they taught me to be vulnerable and honest and unafraid to tell everyone my truth. They taught me to advocate for self-faith and self-acceptance. They showed me how important it is to tell your story, no matter how hard it may be.

They taught me the spell that turns venom into an antidote: *Trust, surrender, open yourself up to the world, and just wait for the revelation to come.*

DAVIS, GIOVANNI, WEST, BROOKS, BUTLER, LORDE, HOOKS, ADICHIE, Shange, Kincaid, Hurston, Naylor, Angelou, Bambara, Walker, Hansberry, Morrison, Smith, Sanchez.

I say those names aloud, and it feels like a chant. A charm. A song. A prayer. A meditation. An invocation.

I say those names aloud and I see the glimmering stretch of words, sentences, chapters, and stories that undulate both backward and forward infinitely throughout time. I see the women whose hands and hearts and immense intelligence and talent wrote those starry pages.

I say those names aloud so they will hold me up, and perhaps even loan me their wings, as I show you my heart, tell you my story, unleash my secrets, and write down my truth.

Thank you for reaching for my book.

PART I

MOTHER TO SON

Well, son, I'll tell you:
Life for me ain't been no crystal stair.
It's had tacks in it,
And splinters,
And boards torn up,
And places with no carpet on the floor—
Bare.
But all the time
I'se been a-climbin' on,
And reachin' landin's,
And turnin' corners,
And sometimes goin' in the dark
Where there ain't been no light.
So boy, don't you turn back.
Don't you set down on the steps
'Cause you finds it's kinder hard.
Don't you fall now—
For I'se still goin', honey,
I'se still climbin',
And life for me ain't been no crystal stair.

LANGSTON HUGHES

CHAPTER ONE

My Book of Bible Stories, Aesop's Fables,
The Berenstain Bears

Cooking was my mother's greatest act of love. The air always smelled like onions and tomatoes, curry powder and thyme. I can see my mom standing in the kitchen, cooking jollof rice. Naturally, Nigeria's best-known dish is rich and complex, with many layers of spices and vegetables. The perfect combination of flavors. My dad is standing next to her, leaning over the wide black pot, inhaling the scent, and snatching up bites.

"Add a little bit more of this," he says, waving at the powdered bouillon. Then he takes another bite and points at a pile of chopped onions and red peppers. "And a bit more of that!"

My mother pokes my father in the soft part of his tummy with her wooden spoon. "Oh, you don't think it's good, eh?" she says. "You think I don't know how to cook?"

"Come on now, Henri." My mother's name is Henrietta

but my father always called her Henri in this loving, sing-song kind of way. "You know you are the best cook in the world. Which is why I have this little belly you are currently poking me in."

They are laughing. They were always laughing back then. My father had a great laugh. He could find the humor in anything, and his laugh—a deep, warm giggle—was the kind that made other people laugh just hearing it, even if they weren't in on the joke. Completely infectious.

My mother mockingly throws up her hands and turns back to the stove. "You are always laughing even when nothing is funny," she says. But I could see from the way her shoulders jumped that she was still laughing, too.

In those days, conversations between my parents sounded like a song to me. Perhaps it was their accents, but there was something melodic in the way they spoke to each other. There was a flow and a rhythm. Their talk was filled with inside jokes and good-natured teasing. They pleased each other, softened in each other's presence. The salty-sweet parley between them made me feel warm, safe, and content.

THE PLAYFUL BANTER BETWEEN MY PARENTS DIFFERED from how my mother engaged with me, her firstborn daughter. Where my mother was raised there is no back-and-forth conversation—in Nigeria children didn't get to have an opinion. They quickly obeyed their parents, finished their food, and prayed for forgiveness. My mother valued obedience and respect over playfulness. So, in our household she and I never engaged in frivolous conversations, only stern instructions. Fix the table. Do your homework. Turn off the television. Read a book. Eat. Always eat. For my mother, raising a well-behaved child was the ultimate goal.

I envied the ease my parents had with each other, but I never felt it extended to me. Unless we were sharing a meal. When my mother asked, "Did you eat?" I always sensed the deep concern in her voice and knew a warm, hearty meal would follow. "Did you eat?" was easily interchangeable with "I love you."

She regularly prepared elaborate dishes: jollof rice, egusi soup, and my favorite dish, moi moi, for dinner. As the aroma of spices filled our tiny two-bedroom apartment, I watched her move steadily about the kitchen. From the cabinet, she would pull out an array of ingredients: black-eyed peas, foil-wrapped cubes of Maggi, and containers filled with tiny smoked dried shrimp. Our freezer was filled with square packages of spinach and fresh goat meat. Mysteriously labeled plastic bags with pungent spices littered our small kitchen counter. I savored the smell of grilled meat slathered with a generous mix of ground peanuts, ginger, and cayenne. The yams in our house were not orangey brown but instead white-fleshed and tough, dull-brown skins that had to be peeled away with a knife. Whenever someone was ill, they were not fed chicken noodle soup. Instead, we slurped the fiery broth of pepper soup, which immediately cleared your sinuses and warmed your chest.

I was accustomed to our meals being colorful and full of unexpected flavors, always paired with white rice. Thick, rich stews that are meant to be eaten with fufu or plantain. All those spices and colors coalesced and brought my palette to life. The nourishment we received went beyond satisfying our hunger. Each plate was a vibrant connection to Nigeria. Every dish said, *Eat this because I love you*. I grew to understand there are numerous ways to express love. Sometimes it is a spoonful of rice or warm glass of milk before bed. My mother's recipes were sacred and held our traditions. In between her loving preparations of food, there was no room to understand the struggles her daughter might be going through. No space to contemplate what it was to be a minority, to grow up Black in America. Instead, she fed and nurtured me the best way she knew how.

My parents survived the Nigerian civil war, also known as the Biafran War. It was a devastating conflict that took place from 1967 to 1970. My Efik and Igbo ancestors were on the losing side. The conflict resulted in significant loss of life, with estimates suggesting that more than a million people died, primarily due to starvation caused by a blockade imposed on Biafra. My father lost his father; my mother was separated from her mother for years. The impact of the war was ingrained in their memories, shaping their identities and influencing their perspectives on the nation's history. The declaration of "no victor, no vanquished" by the Nigerian government was intended to promote reconciliation and unity after the war, but the scars of the conflict lingered for many.

Ten years later, my parents immigrated to the United States, moving through life with raw grief and perseverance.

It has always been unclear to me what they anticipated in coming to the United States. I still cannot comprehend what they lost or who was left behind in order to start a new life. My parents never told me stories about the war. But by the time my brother, Maurice, was born in 1985, they had formed new identities that hinged fully on American aspirations. Because as immigrants, forgetting one's complicated past was normal. Even expected. You landed in the land of the free, home of the brave, and started over. Yet unspoken generational trauma shaped our family dynamic, with secrets and never-ending anxiety. Then there was the concept of being Black in America that carried a complex history and social significance that was rooted in the legacy of slavery, segregation, and systemic racism. The underlying tensions of American society and more awaited my parents. In contrast, I was raised understanding that my Blackness was intricate, ambient, and contained a multitude of definitions.

IT WAS MY FATHER WHO BUILT MY CONFIDENCE AND GREW my curiosity for the world. He named me Glory after his sister, who passed away before my birth. I was always proud to be her namesake. My name evoked an instant joy, reminding people of white church steeples and gospel hymns. When he shouted "Glory" on the playground, people turned and smiled. He was boisterous and loved to tell stories. Sometimes he would tell me tales from his own childhood, about Anansi the spider or Ajapa the tortoise, but usually he would make up his own stories, bringing the inanimate things in our house to life. He'd tell me about the secret thoughts of our dining room chairs, or how there was a whole world turning in the tufts of our red shag rug. Our home became its own kind of adventure. He made me believe there were stories all around us, and that he was able to just snatch them right out of the air.

Even as a little girl, love was a confounding sensation. Yet I always felt the most love with my father. Sometimes I would ask him, "How can you tell when somebody loves you?"

He would gently pull me close and whisper, "You can tell by their smile."

"What do you mean?"

"When someone smiles their love is shining on you. You'll feel warm inside."

My father's smile was wide and generous. He laughed easily, searching for your goodness within your grin. I loved being with him. Sometimes he would tell me to draw a map, and I would color a series of nonsense lines and dots with my crayons, and then he would pretend to read it.

"Let's go outside! Your map says we need to find the tallest tree on the street and then take seven steps to the right!"

Delighted, I would follow him out the door, and we would run to find that tree and take our seven steps. "Now the map says that we must turn around two times and whatever direction we face, walk fifteen steps from there!"

He made it up as he went along, but I always felt like I was the one who was leading the way.

Often, he'd say that the map was directing us to go for a

car ride. He'd buckle me into his old blue Beretta and just drive, telling me a story as we trundled down the road. "I am a pirate, and you are leading me to the treasure! The map says we should go to the mall, but the mall is now a jungle on this deserted island!"

I was enraptured, sitting in the front seat, my legs too short to reach the car floor and just barely able to crane my head up to see out the window, spellbound as my father narrated every turn and swerve. He made everything a grand adventure.

MY FATHER'S INGENUITY AND PERSEVERANCE MADE HIM A natural builder. By trade he was an architect. I remember watching him leave in the morning, carrying his leather briefcase, wearing a tan suit, a striped tie, the tinted sunglasses. Sometimes I would visit him at the office, so tempted by the tiny perfect architectural models of houses and buildings, complete with trees and grass. My hands itched to play with them as if they were dollhouses.

When my father wasn't working, he made sure he was building community. On weekends he would take me to the Nigerian parties hosted on Howard University's campus. At that time, I didn't understand that my father had actually earned his degree at Howard. I just thought it was a space for gatherings. A roomful of colorful Nigerian aunties and uncles. Doctors. Taxi drivers. Accountants. We would spend almost every weekend either at church or at the Blackburn Auditorium, where the Efik cultural association gathered to eat and exchange triumphs and hardships. Sometimes there were parties, filled with food and music and dancing. Sometimes there were fundraisers for students back home in Nigeria or makeshift church services for families who had just immigrated to D.C.

Before every gathering, my mother would dutifully collect bags of rice, kegs of red palm oil, and sacks of garri. There would be huge pots of the yellowish egusi, made of ground melon seeds and vegetables, on the stove. The kitchen would fill with the rich smell of roasted pepper, onion, and tomato. I'd watch her finely chop onions, carefully sauteing the slices in hot oil before adding in her tomato base. The caramelized tendrils gave a spot of sweetness to her signature jollof rice. I can still see the deep red hue of palm oil and how it stained our crème countertops. After cooking for what seemed like hours, heaps of rice and stew would be carefully placed in silver pans and covered with foil.

When my parents were surrounded by fellow Nigerians, I saw them relax in a way they never publicly could otherwise. For my parents and their friends, relocating to a new country had to be an overwhelming experience, marked by cultural differences, language barriers, and the inevitable homesickness. Between the parties and fundraisers, they were building a close-knit community.

MY MOTHER HAD BEEN A PRIMARY SCHOOLTEACHER BEfore she married my father and left Nigeria. She had a keen intellect, a dry sense of humor, and a deep love of words. She became a stay-at-home mom after she and my father were married, and she started teaching me to read as soon as I started to speak. By the time I was three, I was able to pick my way through a book.

The book I remember my mother teaching me from the most was a bright yellow hardback entitled *My Book of Bible Stories* by the Watchtower Bible and Tract Society. It was a large picture book with simplified versions of the classic Bible tales and lavish illustrations that made Adam and Eve look like glamorous creatures with their fur togas and flowing, perfectly styled hair. I am not certain where my mother got the book. We were religious—the church was centered in our lives—but we were not Jehovah's Witnesses. Still, I'm sure that, however it was offered to her, my mother saw no reason to turn down a perfectly good, free book of Bible stories. I remember sitting next to her (always before four o'clock, when *Oprah* came on. *Oprah* was our other religion. We never missed *Oprah*), both of us sunk deep into the brown velvet beanbag chair in our living room and trying not to be distracted by the elaborate illustrations as she helped me sound out the words.

"This is a book of true stories," she read.

My mother's voice was unique. It was soft and accented but filled with conviction. Just listening to her made me want to get the pronunciation right. I loved the repetition, how soothing it was as she would guide me along the page, giving gentle nudges when I hesitated or stumbled. We would stay on a word for as long as it took for me to learn it, figuring out each sound, each part, clapping our hands together for every syllable. My mother loved to sing as well, so sometimes we would sing the syllables to figure out how they came together, what the word would turn out to be.

Because she was an immigrant, my mother was not so caught up in the grammar and rules. She was more concerned that I memorized and understood the alphabet. She wanted me to learn the sounds.

She was incredibly patient. If I faltered over a word, it was no big deal. She would just tell me to try again. And again, and again, if I needed to. When we read together I never felt that she was frustrated by my imperfections or mistakes. This would shift as I got older, but when I was a little person, she offered me this great sense of care. In those early years, I regularly meditated on my mother's voice.

My mother also taught me all fifty states and their capitals. Knowing exactly where in America we were was very important to her, especially in relation to where Africa was. She would take my hand and trace the maps in the atlas, showing me Washington, D.C., and then turning the pages until we found Nigeria. She needed me to understand that we were from both places.

Nigeria was our past, she told me, but America was our future. My mother believed in assimilation. She aspired to live a big life in America. She wanted the classic American dream: the husband, the 2.5 kids, the house, and the white picket fence. And in those days, it all felt within our purview.

———

WE DIDN'T HAVE A LOT OF MONEY. WE LIVED IN A TWO-bedroom apartment with popcorn ceilings and red shag carpet. A beanbag chair. A patchwork couch. My father set up his sound system on a shelf made of cement blocks and boards; I can still see those giant wood-framed speakers with the sharp edges, a turntable, and every Bob Marley album that had ever been released. For the longest time I thought Bob Marley was Nigerian, my father played him so much.

But there was a lot of joy. A sense of achievement. We were moving toward our American dream.

My mother was in her senior year of college in Nigeria when she decided to visit one of her girlfriends in Washington, D.C. That friend took her to a party, and that's where she met my father, also a Nigerian, who was studying urban planning at Howard University.

My dad was immediately smitten with her. She was only in town for another week, but he found a way to see her every day, and when she went back to Nigeria, he started writing to her, sometimes as much as a letter a day. He was certain he had found the woman he was meant to marry.

My mother, unbeknownst to my father, continued to see other men. She liked my father, but she figured since he was in America and she was in Nigeria, it was best to keep her options open. So she was very surprised when, over the Christmas holidays, she was having dinner with a prospective beau when my father knocked on the front door.

My mother thought fast. She rushed her suitor out the back, telling him that her cousin from America had just arrived and it wouldn't do for him to see her alone with a boy.

She then let my father in, and my father, happily oblivious, immediately declared his undying love for her and his desire that she return with him to America and be his wife.

I always laugh and shake my head when my mother tells me what her answer was. "He was handsome, and he was convincing, and he was in the United States, so I thought, *Why not?*"

They didn't know each other at all. What little they did know was almost entirely through letters. They had spent all of a week and a day together before they became engaged. But they were married within a year, and I came along a year after that. My dad graduated from Howard and got his first job at an architecture firm, and my brother Maurice was born five years after me.

AS FAR AS I WAS CONCERNED, MAURICE WAS MY BABY FROM the very beginning. I loved everything about him. I loved his sweet, powdery smell, and his gummy smile, and the way he wrapped his sticky little hands around my neck as I hauled him around the apartment from room to room.

Sometimes, when I was feeling chatty, I would balance him on the couch and take his little face in my hands and smoosh his jaw up and down to make him "talk" to me. We would carry on these long, elaborate conversations.

"So, Maurice, how was your day?"

Hands on his fat little cheeks. "Oh, it was just lovely, Glory. I had some milk and rice cereal for breakfast!"

Hands off his face. "Oh, that sounds very good, Maurice!"

Hands back on. "It was very good! But I made such a mess that Mommy had to give me a bath after breakfast. I didn't like that."

Hands off. "But you needed that bath, you naughty boy!"

When I got tired of talking, I would make up my own stories to tell him. But unlike my dad, I couldn't just snatch them out of the air. I had to sit patiently and think them through and then write them down so I could read them to Maurice later. I liked to start every story with a big, elaborate italic letter just like in the fairy tales I read. I probably spent more time trying to perfect that lettering than I did on planning out my plots, but there was something about writing that first ornate, swoopy letter that opened up my imagination and allowed me to find the rest of my story.

ONCE MAURICE COULD REALLY TALK, MY MOTHER TAUGHT us the Lord's Prayer, and we would recite it out loud to each other every night before we went to bed.

Our Father who art in heaven, hallowed be thy name. Thy kingdom come, thy will be done on earth as it is in heaven . . .

I didn't entirely understand the meaning, but the words, the *sound*—both in my own recitation and echoed in Maurice's sweet, lisping version—lit up my brain with pleasure and peace.

Maurice and I shared a room, and after prayers our mother would let us take turns picking out the nightly bedtime story. Maurice liked Curious George. He loved to laugh at that mischievous little monkey and all the tricks he pulled on the man with the yellow hat. I always asked for Aesop's fables or the Berenstain Bears. I liked stories with a moral at the end. I would listen to my mother read about some character's disastrous mistakes and silently swear to myself that I'd never be so stupid or greedy or disobedient. That I'd be like the competent and wise mama bear, not the bumbling Berenstain papa bear. That I would be the tortoise, not the hare.

Sometimes after my mom would leave the room, Maurice would whisper to me, begging for just one more story. So as quietly as possible, I would recite his favorite. When Maurice had started to crawl and then toddle, and then suddenly started cramming anything and everything he found into his mouth, I wrote him a story, in rhyme, about how he ate all our pets. Mind you, we actually had no pets, but in my story he went from swallowing our goldfish to gulping our turtle to devouring our Saint Bernard.

I never made it all the way through. Somewhere before the ending, Maurice's breathing would grow slow and steady, and I'd know that he'd fallen asleep to the sound of my voice once again.

IN ELEMENTARY SCHOOL, I HAPPILY PLUNGED INTO THE BIGger world. I was in the dance troupe; I was a Brownie and then a Daisy Girl Scout; I volunteered at church. I regularly made the honor roll. And Maurice followed right behind me. We were never apart if we could help it. And our parents praised us and gave us rewards and made us feel seen and special.

My mother got involved in all my school activities. She joined the PTA and offered to care for kids in our neighborhood who didn't have a parent around after school. She cooked and cleaned and made sure that Maurice and I were always neat and tidy.

My father quit his job at the architecture firm, then got a new one. Then quit that job and picked up something else. I didn't understand what drove him, but even as a child I could sense his restlessness, and it sometimes made me uneasy.

Holidays were a huge deal in our family, but our parents had to be creative about how we afforded them. Maurice's birthday was in September, and mine was at the end of December, but in order to save money we were given a joint birthday party every year (on my actual birthdate, poor Maurice!). But I didn't mind sharing. Mom would doll us up. I always had a big pink fluffy dress, and she would do my hair—bangs with curls—and Maurice would be wearing a tiny tuxedo. It was never just hot dogs and fruit punch, either; it was a Nigerian feast. Yellow birthday cake paired with pans of jollof rice, plantains, and puff puff.

AS WE GREW OLDER, THINGS STARTED TO CHANGE BE- tween my parents.

Or maybe things had never been quite as good as I thought they were, and my parents just became less skilled at hiding their problems from us. I don't really know.

My father was an incredibly proud man, and I do know he was facing all sorts of day-to-day racism at work and outside our home. Unlike my mother, he didn't believe in assimilation. He loved Nigeria above all, and he chafed against the way America made him feel small and inconsequential. He started to drink too much, and he was not always faithful to my mom, and my mother was painfully aware of his transgressions.

My mom had no income and limited independence, and when my father betrayed her, she had nowhere to escape to.

The laughter and easy, affectionate words between them disappeared, replaced by tense, hissing conversations.

And then shouting.

And then, worst of all, silence.

MAURICE AND I WOULD HUDDLE IN THE LIVING ROOM AS they fought, trying to distract each other with stupid games or our own little squabbles. When my father would stumble out of the house and my mother would weep in her room, when the silence in the house seemed to press down on us in a way that made us gasp for breath, I would pick up Maurice and put him on the beanbag, then climb in next to him, dragging the big yellow book of Bible stories along with me.

For a moment, we'd just sit side by side, my brother's little shoulder pressed up against mine, feeling the way the beanbag settled to the contours of our bodies and swelled up around us, soft and supportive.

"Ready?" I'd ask Maurice, and he'd nod in return, his big brown eyes locked onto mine.

"This is a book of true stories," I recited, doing my best imitation of my mother's soft, patient voice.

It was my turn to teach someone to read.

CHAPTER TWO

Gary Paulsen, *Hatchet*; Louisa May Alcott, *Little Women*;
Mildred D. Taylor, *Roll of Thunder, Hear My Cry*; Zora Neale
Hurston, *Their Eyes Were Watching God*

My parents finally divorced when I was eight. Every weekend for the next three years, Maurice and I would stay with our father at his townhouse in northern Virginia. The house felt palatial compared to the small two-bedroom apartment our family had crammed ourselves into for the first years of my life. There were multiple bathrooms, a front and back yard, a washer-dryer in our very own basement, a garage for our bikes, and, best of all, for the first time since Maurice had been born, we each had our own rooms.

It was an odd thing, because even though my family was more fractured than ever, I look back on that time and the house we shared with our father as the closest version of a true home that I have ever experienced.

Maurice and I would spend the day exploring the neighborhood and then ride home as it got dark, simply dropping our bikes on the front lawn without having to lug them up six flights of stairs or worry about them being stolen. Occasionally, our father half-heartedly attempted to get us to do yardwork—handing us a rake or a push mower—which was fun until the novelty wore off. But if we were reluctant, he never insisted. I could sit under a tree in the yard when it was nice outside, or curled up on the bed in my room when it rained, and spend the whole day reading. No one would bother me. It was *Leave It to Beaver*. It was what I had always imagined middle-class America to be. I remember walking through the house for the first time, my father proudly pointing out every little detail, and thinking, *So, this is how white people live.*

Even though my parents were separated, my mother actually picked out all the furniture and supervised the decoration of that house. She made sure it was a suitable home for her children. And I think this gave my father hope. I think he wanted—and expected—her to come back to him someday. This house would be *their* house. Our family would be reunited. He knew he had messed up. He understood that he had hurt her. And now, every little thing he did felt like it was in service of making things up to her.

I was perfectly content to believe that they would find each other again, but in the meantime, I didn't actually mind their separation so much. They had been unhappy when they lived together, and the space between them now felt cordial and healing for us all. I thought I had the best of both worlds: the school I loved in our old neighborhood with my mother, and this perfect new house filled with privacy and space, toys and books, lawn and garden, with my father. I sometimes worried about my dad, thinking he must have been lonely while Maurice and I were gone during the week. I wondered what he did in that big house all by himself. But mostly, I moved between my homes and parents with remarkable ease.

My mother had created the room of my young dreams: pink and white, with a canopy bed and a matching desk and bureau. My father spoiled me by buying me all the latest toys. Not just one but two Kenya dolls, the kind that had a button on her back that could be pressed to grow her long, dark curls all the way down to her toes. A stack of Fashion Plates that could be mixed and matched and interchanged within a plastic drawing tablet so that I could take my colored pencils and shade out endless variations of stylish outfits. I had a closet full of pretty dresses. Reams of stationery and multicolored construction paper, tubs of crayons and markers. And, best of all, tower upon tower of books, which were all the more valuable because I knew my father would actually allow me the time and space to read them.

Privacy also meant a chance for me to try things I never would have dared to explore at my mother's apartment. My father's good nature and warm support allowed me to be bold. More than one bathroom meant I could lock myself up, draw a fluffy and fragrant bubble bath, slather my face with St. Ives apricot scrub, and attempt to shave my legs for the first time. Not knowing any better, I used my father's safety razor on my dry legs, almost instantly peeling a swath of skin half an inch wide and three inches long off my left shin. My father, hearing my cries, burst into the bathroom and looked panicked at first, seeing the gore. I had managed to splatter blood from what seemed like floor to ceiling. But as soon as he realized what had happened, he tenderly wrapped me up in a towel and took me onto his lap. He didn't shame or scold me. He just helped me bandage my leg as he commented with a soft laugh that I must truly be growing into a woman to try such womanly things.

My mother started dating the man who would become her second husband about two years after she and my father split up. A good friend of hers introduced them. He was Nigerian, too, but from a different tribe than ours, not even from the same region. He drove a cab. He was tall and puritanical and grim—especially compared with my softer, sweeter father. He never even bothered to try to win over Maurice or me. He was stern and cold and judgmental from the moment we met him. I was instructed to call him "Uncle," and every time I said it I tasted dirt in my mouth.

I thought he was temporary. Maybe even someone my mother had chosen just to make my father jealous. I couldn't fathom that she would pick a man like him over a man like my dad. Unlike my father, whose warmth and humor had always tempered my mother's tendency to be rigid and unyielding when it came to Maurice and me, "Uncle" was an extreme traditionalist who believed children existed to silently serve and defer to the adults in their lives. He was a strict Muslim, and he twisted his religious beliefs into proof of his right to dominate those around him. He insisted that any unprompted question from children, even the most innocent, should be interpreted as pure disrespect to adults.

He encouraged my mother to be unsparing and wasted no time in critiquing every large and small thing that he felt Maurice and I did wrong. All with a disgusted half sneer on his face.

AFTER "UNCLE" APPEARED IN OUR LIVES, THE WEEKENDS AT my father's became even more important. They were not just about dividing our time between our parents; they were now a desperately needed respite from the nearly constant criticism and judgment, from the insistence that I shut my mouth and do as I was told. My father's house became the only place where I could break my own silence without being punished. Where funny stories were still told. Where jokes were made. Where laughter rang out. Where my curiosity and opinions were encouraged and praised rather than seen as terrible flaws in my personality. My father didn't value or desire my obedience. He told me that he loved my quick and inquisitive mind. He smiled at me when I chattered at him, his eyes crinkling with pleasure. He never looked at me with anything less than warmth and pride. I knew, without a doubt, that I was both valued and loved under my father's roof.

My father was aware that my mother was seeing another man. But I was absolutely certain that my dad would never give up on her, or on us as a family. I knew that it was just a matter of time before he would step up and insist that my mother leave this terrible man behind, and we would all be rightfully together again.

———

ONE FRIDAY NIGHT WHEN I WAS ELEVEN, MY MOTHER WAS driving Maurice and me to our father's house as she always did. The drive was long—almost an hour—but I didn't mind because it gave me a good stretch of uninterrupted time to read in the car.

On this particular day, I was reading *Hatchet* by Gary Paulsen. It was an assignment for school. I had resisted it a bit before I started reading—I preferred to choose my own books—but after the first few pages, *Hatchet* sucked me in entirely. It was the story of a young boy who was the sole survivor of a plane crash and had to find a way to stay alive in the wilderness until he could be rescued. The fact that this character's parents were also recently divorced spoke to me, of course, but there was something particularly compelling about his struggle to survive.

Since my mother's boyfriend had entered our lives, I had been ardently consuming survival stories. Books about overcoming hardship, books about kids in unusually difficult circumstances, books that explored all the ways that people in powerless situations could find a sense of control and autonomy. *Hatchet* fit perfectly into this matrix: the worst of circumstances combined with an astounding will to live.

"Oh no," said my mother from behind the wheel. "What is this?" And then she swore softly under her breath.

My mother never swore. Hearing her do so jerked me from the dreamy world of my book and made me realize that we had arrived at my father's house. I turned my head to look out the window.

All my father's furniture and household items were sitting curbside and scattered across the front lawn.

"Stay in the car," my mother told Maurice and me.

She climbed out of the driver's seat and picked her way through the maze of household detritus, heading for the front door.

I felt my stomach contract with fear as I cataloged all the familiar items stacked up in the street. It wasn't just my father's things. There were my bed and mattress. The posters from my bedroom wall. My Kenya dolls. Maurice's Hot Wheels set. A stack of my books.

My mother peered through a window and then knocked on the door.

No one answered.

She knocked again, but louder. She tried the knob, but it was locked.

I watched her return. She didn't bother to stop and look at anything. She just marched straight through and got back into the car.

"He's gone," she said.

And then she started up the engine, saying nothing more.

I stayed quiet, but every part of me wanted to wail in panic as we drove away. At first my brain snagged on the loss of my *things*. It had felt like an unimaginable luxury to finally have a room of my own, and I didn't want to leave any of that behind. I wanted my bed and my books and my stuffed animals. My dolls and my games and my Fashion Plates. I wanted to insist that my mother turn the car around so we could salvage it all.

My brain had already begun its work of minimizing and

compartmentalizing. *He's gone,* I would think, and then something inside me would quickly change the subject, fixating on the lamp I'd really loved or the little desk where I'd sat to write in my journal.

But he *was* gone. My father was gone. Without a word to my mother or Maurice or me.

Eventually we found out that he had moved back to Nigeria.

In the beginning, very occasionally, there would be a quick and awkward phone call from him, but those eventually petered off, and more than ten more years would pass before I would see or hear from my father again. The man who had once meant everything to me.

THE LOSSES BEGIN TO PILE UP SOON AFTER. I HAD A BEST friend named Charisse. We did everything together. We would dress alike, she would help me care for my brother, we were in Girl Scouts together, we were constantly in and out of each other's homes. I thought of her as my platonic soulmate, my twin. And then she and her family moved away. Far away. And in those days there was no texting or Zooming. Even long-distance phone calls were forbiddingly expensive, so she, too, was just gone. I was devastated in that way only an eleven-year-old girl who lost her best friend can be.

Not long after that, my mother announced that she was pregnant, and that she and her boyfriend were engaged to be married.

I know now that she had her reasons. All of her friends from Nigeria, our greater community, were still married, so there was a certain social pressure. And since my father was truly gone, my mother was incredibly worried about the possibility of being deported. And, of course, there was a baby on the way. But her boyfriend felt dangerous to me, and that danger felt even sharper since my father had disappeared. My mother willingly accepted his authority over us. Now she had no other, softer, parent to balance her out. No one else she had to answer to.

And Maurice and I had absolutely no one to turn to for protection.

We moved to a big apartment complex called Shirley Park. It was another cramped two-bedroom apartment, but now he lived with us, too. The move also meant I would be attending a new school in the fall. More loss: our old apartment, the old neighborhood, my school and friends, the relative peace that had once been a part of our home, any hope for my mother's happiness. All gone as well.

IN THIS HAZE OF DEFICIENCY, I TURNED TO THE ONLY PLACE that I knew would help.

Each day during that summer, my brother and I headed to the Arlington public library. It was massive, like its own small town. And during that time, that hushed, beautiful building felt more like home than our actual home did.

Besides books, the library granted us uninhibited space. We could walk among and between the stacks, touch book spines, and hide in endless corners. My brother would read his picture books while I did homework or wrote in my journal or sussed out the next book I was going to read.

Maurice and I shared a mutual devotion to each other. As the older sister, I was a makeshift guardian and automatic best friend. We would wander the library together, gathering our books and finding just the right space to settle down. If we lost sight of each other in the hallways, we instinctively called out "brother" and "sister," patiently waiting for the other to reappear.

Together we read piles and piles of books that made us want to see other places, do other things, be all the other possible versions of ourselves we read about in those pages. We held hands, caught our breath, and sank deep into the words and chapters, uninterrupted for hours. Reading allowed us to briefly change our circumstances. We would daydream, pretending to live in a big, fancy house where we had our own separate bedrooms again. At the library our parents were no longer divorced. There was no evil new stepfather. No missing father. No new baby on the way. With our borrowed books we created simple realities and immersed ourselves in new worlds, too. Together we read *Corduroy, Charlie and the Chocolate Factory,* and *Charlotte's Web*. Fighting Maurice's short attention span, I read everything out loud, intent on figuring out the lesson in each story: Great things often start off small. Don't waste a moment in self-doubt. Try to be optimistic even when things look hopeless.

We became so comfortable in that haven that one day I found myself slipping off my shoes, forgetting that I was not in my bedroom. My brother and I had sprawled out on the grayish carpet in the children's section, Maurice absentmind-edly reading *Where the Wild Things Are* as I thumbed through a tattered copy of *Little Women*. I quickly decided that Jo was my favorite March sister. Although I knew it was against the rules, I secretly underlined her sentences with a dull num-ber 2 pencil, pressing down hard under the quote "I like good strong words that mean something."

Here were more survivors. *Little Women*'s protagonists were imperfect, complex girls with rich inner lives. They all pursued different paths. Meg, the eldest, became a wife and mother. Jo desired to be a great writer. Beth was painfully shy and virtuous. Amy, the youngest, had artistic ambitions. Missing a father for most of the book, and with a mother who was often gone or busy, the older sisters spent much of their time caring for the younger ones. The story was set in 1861, and the sisters clearly looked nothing like me, but nonetheless I was fixated. Their triumphs and heartbreaks inspired my preteen gumption. Years before I discovered Sula Peace or Shug Avery, Jo March was my favorite fictional her-oine. She was always creating something, defining herself in a world determined to box her in. Like so many girls who grow up wanting to write and push against social conven-tions, Jo's independence and rebellion felt plausible. It was my first and most meaningful encounter with a character who was free-spirited and unafraid. Jo never fell into the trap of perfectionism, and she, too, loved reading along with the heartening process of creating imaginary worlds. I found myself lost in her desires, less aware of my childhood insecu-rities. My stutter. My weight. My unruly hair.

My loneliness. My losses.

When I glanced out a window and noticed that the sky was turning dark outside, I poked Maurice and told him to gather up his things. I carried the well-loved hardcover of *Little Women* to the library circulation desk, Maurice following behind holding on to *Alexander and the Terrible, Horrible, No Good, Very Bad Day*. The librarian was kind and familiar with our round, brown faces. She gently reminded us to treat our borrowed books with care.

JUNE JORDAN WROTE,

> It seems obvious that the best way to bring people into the library is to bring them in: Bring them in as writers, as thinkers, as readers. I think of the library as a sanctuary from the spectacle, from the alienation, from the unnamed, and the seeming unnameable. A library is where you keep records of involvement, the glorious and ugly tangling of the human spirit with what we meet, what we see. A library is where you keep records of human experience humanly defined: That means humanly evaluated and that means life worded into ideas living people can use.
>
> People belong in such a sanctuary. Bring them in. Bring the children into the library as writers; that will help them to think, and that will lead them to read.

Whenever we stepped out of the bright, air-conditioned library into the hazy, twilight heat of the street, I felt an inevitable sense of dread. We were leaving our safe haven, our very own sanctuary. My mother worked long shifts as a nurse—three to eleven, most nights—so it was usually up to me to make sure that Maurice and I made it home, did our homework, had dinner, and put ourselves to bed. Leaving the library meant stepping into the reality of responsibility and taking care of other people along with myself. I hated the fact that Mom had to work so much. I wanted her to be there to make us dinner and greet us when we got home. I didn't like fending for ourselves, but I also didn't like to be alone with my mother's boyfriend.

We climbed up the hill to our house, our backpacks weighed down with our library books, and came home to our empty apartment. I turned on lights, and cooked something that smelled good, and reminded Maurice to take a bath and brush his teeth. I did my best to make things warm and safe and snug. Then, after we changed into our night clothes, we climbed into our little beds, and I read to him first, all about Alexander's disaster of a day, until I heard his breath go slow and steady and looked to see that his eyes had fallen shut. Then I opened my copy of *Little Women* and picked up where I had left off.

MY MOTHER MADE A FRIEND IN OUR NEW APARTMENT building, a woman named Elizabeth Woldemichael who lived in apartment 7 to our apartment 5, both of us on the third floor. Ms. Woldemichael had emigrated from Eritrea, in East Africa, around the same time my mother had come to the United States from Nigeria. She was a single mom with twin girls, Ida and Selma.

"You should be friends with them," said my mother. "They're just your age and such nice girls. So smart and polite!"

My mother was hovering in my bedroom door as I was reading *Roll of Thunder, Hear My Cry* and doing my best to ignore her. If I couldn't be at the library, this was the next best place, lying on my bed, propped up on my elbows, reading, preferably with the door shut.

"Glory? Are you listening? These girls live only two doors down. You're lucky to have them so close. If you get to know them now, you will have nice friends at your new school when you start in the fall."

I rolled my eyes. I didn't want new friends. I was still grieving Charisse and all the friends I had left behind at my old school. What was the point of bringing new people into your life if they were only going to leave anyway?

My mother badgered me all summer, but I was resolute in ignoring her. Whenever I happened to pass the sisters in our hallway or outside the building, I would pointedly look away.

Instead, I haunted the library, and if I couldn't be there, I stayed in my room and read, doing my best to block out the noise of my mother and her new husband arguing over . . . everything, really.

———

BECAUSE I STILL HARBORED FANTASIES OF MY PARENTS RE-uniting, of my father returning from Nigeria and making it all better, I would not have been happy even if my mother had chosen a good man to be with. But this was not a good man. Even as a young, snarky teen, I could tell, *this was bad.* His rigidness plagued our household. There was always a sense of agitation—jeering glances and constant disapproval. My body tensed as he creeped outside of my bedroom door. The emotional abuse was always present but harder to define at the time. He demanded to be in control of my mother. All I could do was watch helplessly. I was too shielded and inexperienced to understand things like bills or green cards or any of the many reasons a woman might think she needed a man in the house at any cost. I just knew that our new home was not a safe space and that my mother's marriage was not going to be a happy or nurturing relationship. I could tell that something essential was being forced. That there was oppression and danger in our house.

But, of course, I was not allowed to voice this fear.

OTHER THAN *LITTLE WOMEN, ROLL OF THUNDER, HEAR MY CRY* was the book I loved best that summer. The novel, written by Mildred D. Taylor, is set in Mississippi during the Great Depression, against a backdrop of racial tension and segregation in the American South. At ten years old, Cassie is a strong and determined character, especially considering the challenges she faces in a white-dominated world. I immediately recognized and admired her outspoken nature and self-confidence. Despite their obvious differences, Cassie Logan and Jo March felt essentially the same to me. They were both strong, outspoken girls who cared for their siblings. They made mistakes, but they kept their integrity, no matter what they were faced with. I recognized them both. They spoke to me, right from the page, and as far as I was concerned, they were all the friends I needed.

I liked that Cassie was Black, and I recognized and responded to the Black pride that filled that particular story. But unlike many of the Black women who later joined the Well-Read Black Girl Book Club, I hadn't really been craving that reflection of myself in the books I read. Arlington in the early 1990s was a hub for immigrants and very multicultural. I was lucky to be surrounded by Black people. I never found myself in spaces that were dominated by white people. I never felt different or alone in that way. I wasn't searching out these books to see myself reflected because I was already surrounded by people who looked like me. I didn't need that kind of shoring up.

What I was truly interested in were stories of children who were in peril and somehow made it out. I needed to read to understand survival. I wanted to know how you developed character, how to face adversity and overcome it and still come out as an intact person. I wasn't looking for a reflection; I was looking for practical advice. I liked *Hatchet* because it read almost like an instructional pamphlet on how to survive in the wilderness. After reading that book, I truly felt that I could make it on my own if I ever crashed into a remote Canadian forest. I liked *Little Women* and *Roll of Thunder, Hear My Cry* because those girls were struggling, they had burdens and responsibilities beyond their years, and they still found a way to be emotionally fulfilled. They found a way out of the danger that surrounded them.

In fact, the last thing I was looking for in these books was a mirror image. I wasn't much attracted to who I saw in the looking glass in those days. After my father left, I began to dismiss the fact that I was Nigerian. My father had always been the one to keep that part of our heritage alive. He had made sure that Maurice and I knew exactly where we were from and who we were. He had taught me to be proud to be Nigerian. But now, with him so suddenly and brutally gone, I didn't want to be African anymore. For all his love of our country, he had spoiled it when he chose Nigeria over me and Maurice. I believed he had rejected me, so I began to reject what had been most essential about him. To wish myself into a new, non-African version of Glory.

I liked the idea of Cassie's southern American Blackness. It felt like a culture I could aspire to, and so much easier to explain than being from Nigeria. I liked the fact that her family owned and valued their land above almost anything. The description of their physical home and the landscape around it spoke to the part of me that had been uprooted over and over, the little girl who saw her things scattered across the lawn and into the street. I wanted a *real* home. I longed to own something that couldn't be taken away. A place where people stayed put. And this idea gave me something to look forward to, an image to move toward, the possibility of what would come if I could just find a way to navigate through those hard times.

———

MANY YEARS LATER, MY FATHER WOULD LEAVE A HOUSE HE built in Nigeria to Maurice and me. Neither of us are currently able to live in it. It sits empty most of the time. It was something he had been determined to do—find a way to leave us a piece of land. He sometimes hinted that it was the main reason he had returned to Nigeria. He, too, had apparently felt the need for *home.* But of course, he and I had both misunderstood the concept. It wasn't necessarily a geographical place we were longing for. What was the point of a grand house if it was empty of the people you loved? Maurice and I would have rather had our father than this inheritance. We would trade this house without a thought if it meant just a few moments more with him.

I DRESSED CAREFULLY ON THE FIRST DAY OF SIXTH GRADE. I was meticulous about my curly roller-set bangs and my matching hair bow, pristine sneakers, and scrunchy socks. I was not happy, exactly—I never felt much happiness in my current situation—but I did feel prepared.

Except that I was not. I was cluelessly standing at the wrong bus stop, and probably would have stood there all day if not for Ida and Selma—the girls my mother had been trying to pair me with all summer—who apparently decided to forgive me for snubbing them every chance I got.

"Hey," one of them said as they walked by. "You're at the wrong bus stop. This is for public buses, not the school bus."

I felt my face burn. To me, there was no feeling worse than ignorance.

The other sister smiled at me. "Do you want to walk with us?"

And just like that, we became best friends. A friendship that would last for the rest of our lives.

Ida and Selma were not readers. They were athletes and dancers, at ease in their bodies in a way that I envied. Ida was also an incredible artist who could bring anything to life with just a few quick strokes of her pencil, and Selma was one of those girls who excelled at almost anything she tried. They did well in school, but they were both amused and mystified by the idea of reading for pleasure. They sometimes liked to tease me about my reading, making gentle fun when I stuck my nose in a book all through our free period. And if I would try to tell them about something I had read, they would politely entertain the conversation—but then change the subject as soon as they could. That said, I never felt like they wanted me to change. They didn't make me feel awkward or geeky for reading, or question why I spent so much time in the library. Instead, they just accepted me as I was, folded me into their friendship, invited me to be part of their two-person dance team (which we immediately re-christened Twin Plus, me being the Plus in the equation) no matter my questionable dance skills. They forced me out of my room, out of my head, and into a more joyful place.

The twins' apartment was a mirror image of ours. Two bedrooms. Small and cramped. But it felt like a different world. Their family was from Eritrea, East African as opposed to our West, and they practiced a beautiful, traditional coffee ritual called Buna, so that every time you walked into their house you were engulfed in the rich, comforting scent of roasting coffee beans. Their mom was the only parent in the household, but she had seven brothers. And all those brothers had children, so the apartment was invariably filled with noise and laughter and the kind of family that always made room for solitary outsiders like my brother and me.

Their mother worked as much as mine but kept more regular hours, so that she was usually home when we got back from school each day. Ms. Woldemichael was funny and warm and doted on her girls. She was an amazing cook. I still can't eat Ethiopian food in a restaurant without thinking about all the ways it falls short of hers. From the very beginning, she welcomed me—and not long after that, Maurice as well—with a wide-open door and a huge smile. If something bad was going on in my house—if my mom was working late or Maurice or I were in trouble—we would simply walk two doors down into what felt like a safer, brighter, and better place.

Ms. Woldemichael loved my mother, too. My mother called her Lizzy, the only person I ever heard use that nickname with her. They would sit and talk over coffee in the kitchen while the twins and I endlessly practiced our dance routines in their living room, forcing Maurice to be our captive audience. I felt great relief knowing that my mother had found something like the kind of support I had. That she had someone she could depend on, a friend who drew her out and listened and accepted her for who she was. They covered for each other, traded childcare, Ms. Woldemichael bringing us into her home and my mother taking us out into the bigger world. My mom would take us on field trips—the Smithsonian, the zoo, to Six Flags, or out to eat at a buffet. (My mother loved a buffet—so cost-effective for kids!) It was only years later that I realized that the reason she insisted on taking us places was that she probably needed to get out of our house—and away from her husband—as much as I did.

So maybe I wasn't Jo March after all. Maybe I was more like Laurie, that lonely, dreamy, sad boy who lived next door, missing his parents, gazing longingly into the Marches' happier home. And maybe the twins were my March girls, drawing me out, making me laugh and dance, teaching me to survive, and insisting that there was no joy in hiding myself away.

If it hadn't been for Ida and Selma, I don't know how I would have ever made it through my mother's wedding day.

My mother was quite pregnant by then, and they were getting married at City Hall, but I think my mother wanted it to feel like a more sacred event. She wore a boxy ivory-colored brocade dress with little pearl buttons. It had to be let out to accommodate her pregnant belly, and, combined with her white pill hat and veil, I remember thinking that it looked like nothing so much as an Easter dress that one of the older aunties might wear to church. "Uncle" looking ludicrously dressed up for a City Hall wedding, wore a white tuxedo that made my mother's conservative outfit seem even more matronly in comparison. Maurice wore a matching suit to the groom's, but he was much cuter, of course. And

Ida, Selma, and I, who were serving as bridesmaids (even though it turned out that none of the children would be allowed into City Hall for the actual ceremony), were pressed into matching puritanical peach-colored dresses with wide, floppy collars, white tights, and white buckled church shoes.

I should have been panicking. This was the last day things could still be saved. The last day my father might return, swooping in, straight from Africa, laying claim to my mother and me and Maurice, and banishing this horrible man back to wherever he'd originally come from. Of course, I knew, logically, that my mother was having another man's child, but somehow even that seemed manageable as long as my mother didn't actually utter the words "I do."

Every moment that ticked closer to the wedding should have felt like a doomsday clock to me, but I actually wasn't thinking about that. I wasn't thinking about the permanence of what was about to happen or the unlikelihood of my father finally showing up. Instead, I was clowning around with Ida and Selma, all three of us crammed into their mother's bedroom, getting ready for the dreaded wedding. We had been forced into dresses we hated, but as a compromise, we'd been told we could do our own hair and even apply a little makeup.

When I was growing up, my mother was an extremely well-groomed woman. Her nails were always done. Her hair was always coiffed. But she had never found the time to teach me to take care of myself in the same way. I watched her put on lipstick or pluck her eyebrows, shave her legs, but that didn't translate into actually knowing the proper way to apply any of those things to my own face or body. I had pored through back issues of *Seventeen* magazine and tried to imagine myself amid those blond, snake-hipped white models, learning to properly use eyeliner or jauntily tipping my beret just so. But none of that helped as I leaned into the mirror between my two best friends, attempting to apply mascara without looking like a raccoon.

Ida and Selma, thrilled that they were allowed to choose their own hairstyle, had gone way overboard. They both had gorgeous curly hair, long enough to reach their butts, and they were not afraid of being extra. Selma had decided on tight cornrows that plummeted down her back. Ida had parted her hair down the middle and pulled it back to the base of her neck into a bun so enormous that I actually wondered how she was holding her head up straight. I had used my trusty pink spongy curlers to create a modified bob with dented waves and big fat curly bangs.

We all thought we looked marvelous.

"Does this look right?" I asked as I smoothed on some of their mother's cherry-colored lipstick.

Their mother was with my mom, helping her get dressed, so we were alone in their apartment.

Ida squinted at me. "It's nice, but you got some on your teeth."

I ran my tongue over my front teeth and then grimaced into the mirror. "How about now?"

Selma nodded. "Good. You look good. What kind of blush should we use, do you think?"

We were all bent over their mother's dressing table, examining the various creams and powders, when my lips began to tingle. I wrinkled my nose, not wanting to touch my mouth and mess up the lipstick.

"Oh my God, Glory!" gasped Selma. "What's wrong with your mouth?"

"What?" I slurred. My lips suddenly felt numb and puffy.

"Whoa, girl!" said Ida. "Look at your lips!"

I jerked my head up, looking into the mirror, and stared. My lips were almost twice their normal size.

"Oh no," I said. But it came out more like "Ew new" because I could no longer form my lips into an O shape.

"Quick!" yelped Selma. "Get it off!"

Ida ran into the bathroom and returned with a roll of toilet paper, unraveling a handful as she came toward me. "Here!" she said, thrusting it at me.

I scrubbed at my rubbery lips. "Ew new," I moaned. "Ew new!"

"Get it all!" said Ida. "Did you get it all?"

I held out the toilet tissue, covered in pink smears. "I dewn't knew! Did I? Ew new! My mewm is gewing to kill me!"

Ida and Selma stared at me for a moment and then burst into roars of laughter.

"Hey!" I protested. "It's newt funny!"

They laughed even harder. Doubling over, holding each other up.

"Oh my God." Ida took a deep breath. "Oh my God. I'm sorry. I'm sorry." She started laughing all over again.

Selma looked up at me, her eyes streaming with tears. "You really do look better already," she giggled. "I swear."

I shook my head at her. But then I grinned—or at least I tried to.

MY LIPS SHRUNK BACK DOWN TO SIZE BEFORE THE WED-ding. There were prayers and more prayers before the ceremony. I remember peeking through my lashes at Ida and Selma. Their family didn't attend church or a mosque, so I was worried they would feel uncomfortable or awkward, but they both looked relaxed and properly solemn.

Couples were only allowed to bring in one witness, so all the kids stood on the street outside City Hall while my mother and her new husband and the twins' mother went in for the ceremony. I held Maurice's hand and tried to play it cool as I casually looked around, giving in to a little daydream that, just maybe, I'd see our father running down the street, ready to object.

But, of course, he was nowhere to be found.

"I hate this dress," said Selma, violently yanking at the collar.

"We look like we're in a Thanksgiving pageant," said Ida. "Playing the pilgrims."

"Good sir," joked Selma, "wouldst thou please pass the turkey?"

I laughed at their clowning. It was true. These horrible dresses; my mother's thick, severe, church-lady ensemble; her new husband's ridiculous tuxedo; Maurice's matching outfit—they all combined to make the day feel like we were playing dress-up. A costume party. Pretend.

Maybe none of this is real, I thought.

Maybe my mother wasn't really marrying a man I hated and who I knew hated me twice as much right back. Maybe I wasn't now stuck with a stepfather who made me feel small and ugly and wrong. Maybe I could close my eyes and open them again, and instead of City Hall and a stupid peach pilgrim dress, I would see my father's house and my old room and my father himself, holding his arms out to me with nothing but pride in his eyes.

I squeezed my eyes shut and then opened them.

Peach dress. Busy street. Sun making me sweat my curls into frizz. My little brother, grasping my damp hand in his.

And my friends, patiently waiting with me. Not going anywhere.

CHAPTER THREE

Zora Neale Hurston, *Their Eyes Were Watching God*; Maya Angelou, *I Know Why the Caged Bird Sings* and *The Complete Collected Poems of Maya Angelou*; Frederick Douglass, *Narrative of the Life of Frederick Douglass, an American Slave. Written by Himself*

I started reading Zora Neale Hurston's 1937 classic *Their Eyes Were Watching God* just after my youngest brother, Tunde, was born. It was a leap for me, reading-wise—a decidedly adult book that Oprah had recommended on her show (always, always, we return to Oprah) that was filled with the kind of vivid, difficult language that forced me to slow down and take each sentence in small bites. There was a rigor to this book that I hadn't experienced before. It was the first time I had really noticed or thought about the voice of a book, and it wasn't an easy voice for me to understand. It took such energy and willpower to parse what Hurston was saying in her carefully woven southern dialect, but that effort and struggle to get through the text gave me a sense of accomplishment. It brought me back to that southern world that I had first read about in *Roll of Thunder, Hear My Cry*. It made me long for a place beyond the small and limited one I knew so well.

In Janie Crawford, I found my strongest survivor so far: a woman who bucked against society, who bounced from one tragic situation to the next (The abusive husbands! The storm! The dog bite! Rabies!), and ultimately found a way to move beyond them and be truly happy.

The book begins with Janie telling her story to her best friend, Pheoby Watson, and I understood this part instinctively. Janie talked to Pheoby the same way that I confided in Ida and Selma. Though rather than recounting my history as Janie did, I had a habit of telling stories and making things up—daydreaming. I would spin tales of what my life could be if I had the power to fix it.

Years later, I would read the book out loud in its entirety while standing in my dorm room, still desperate to understand the book's magnificence and capture Janie Crawford's gentle southern drawl: "Love is lak da sea. It's uh movin' thing, but still and all, it takes its shape from de shore it meets, and it's different with every shore."

Something about the book soothed me, each chapter reminding me that love did not care about my past, my age, or even my mistakes. I read as Janie grew from a vibrant teenage girl to a sophisticated woman; I witnessed her life unfold in the story. And oddly enough, the painful parts—the moments when she yearned for unconditional love, losing her beloved Tea Cake, and the terrifying storm that changed her destiny—greatly inspired me. As I read Hurston's words, I felt a newfound consciousness emerge:

There is a basin in the mind where words float around on thought and thought on sound and sight. Then there is a

depth of thought untouched by words, and deeper still a
gulf of formless feelings untouched by thought."

I longed to enter this alluring space where I would freely
follow my instincts. Could I live my life as Janie Crawford
did, filled with my fair share of pain and victory? Did I have
the power to choose my own path?

THERE CERTAINLY WASN'T MUCH CHOICE IN MY LIFE AT
that time. My new little brother was handed over to me in a
way that Maurice had never been. Now that I was thirteen,
my mother, who was still working late and double shifts,
and my stepfather, who just didn't seem to feel that his son
was his responsibility, judged me plenty old enough to care
for an infant. I changed diapers and helped with his milk
bottles. And every day after school, I would trudge over and
collect him from the babysitter's before coming home to feed
him and Maurice their dinners and then put the both of
them to bed.

Anytime I was out a little late with my friends or brought
home a less-than-stellar grade from school (meaning anything less than an A), my stepfather would tell me I was
doomed to be a teen mom. "Mark my words," he'd hiss at
me. "Lazy, irresponsible girl. Knocked up by fifteen. You've
got that slutty look about you."

This both enraged and terrified me. I was a good girl. A
sweet-natured, churchgoing teenager whose biggest rebellion consisted of trying to steal a little extra time to read.
Taking care of Maurice and now Tunde gave me a very clear

idea of how hard being a teen mother might be. I couldn't stand the judgmental looks that I got around the neighborhood when I was carrying baby Tunde with me. The way that certain people shook their heads and sucked their teeth at me. They were the same looks that my stepfather gave me whenever I fell under his gaze. And I hated him for twisting the responsibility that I felt toward my brothers into something that felt wrong and shameful.

"He's my brother," I hastily told anyone who asked and even those who didn't.

Despite all that, I adored Tunde. He was a bright, happy infant, and having him placed in my care fired up my nascent maternal instincts. Babies are so fragile, I realized, and needed so much attention, and Tunde's presence changed me. I was determined to be attentive and attuned to his needs and give him everything he was supposed to have, even if it cost me my free time, my space to dream and read.

Seeing how much hands-on care and effort a baby demanded also made me look back on Maurice when he had been a baby and worry that I hadn't done enough. I recognized that I was lucky to have been born in a time when my parents' marriage was still fairly new and intact. I had received a foundation of love and attachment—fond attention from my father, hands-on care from my mother—that Maurice, and later Tunde, would lack. I think I had sensed this even when I was small, lugging Maurice around when he was half my size. But a six-year-old cannot be responsible for a baby's emotional development, and as I stepped in as a second mother to Tunde, I felt the sharp pangs of what Maurice had missed.

Tunde was precocious and alert and keen. He was so lively, with bright, focused eyes that made me feel, even before he could speak, that he could understand everything I said to him. I would play the same game I had with Maurice, taking his chin in my hand and carrying on conversations. I wanted him to hurry up and talk to me. I wanted to know what he thought, what he felt. Nobody in the house ever asked me how I was doing. Instead, they told me what I should do. So I always asked Maurice, "How was your day? How was school? How do you feel?" And I couldn't wait until I could have that same essential conversation with Tunde.

WHEN I READ AN AUTHOR, I FELT COMPELLED TO READ NOT only everything they had written but also as much as I could that had been written *about* them.

I found that Zora Neale Hurston did not live an easy life. She lost her mother young and as a teen was turned out of the house by her father. She fought to complete her delayed education, eventually earning an associate's degree from Howard University and becoming the first Black woman to attend and graduate from Barnard College. Her brilliance was recognized in her lifetime with scholarships and publications and a teaching position at North Carolina College for Negroes. She collaborated with Langston Hughes and was a vital part of the Harlem Renaissance. But by the time she died, she was impoverished, working as a maid, and had been forgotten by most of the reading public.

Still, there was something about the way that, like Janie, she had insisted on following her own path that inspired thirteen-year-old me. The fact that her fortune was in decline in the end made me angry and frustrated that such a brilliant mind had been cast aside, but the gift of her posthumous resurgence, led by Alice Walker, made me see yet another way that the wheel of fate turns. What felt like an ending actually was not. Even after Hurston left this earth, her words, her ideas, and her books lingered on and somehow, like the best kind of luck, fell into my hands just when I needed them most.

I remember rocking Tunde in my bedroom, one arm full of baby, one hand propping up the book that I read over his small, sweet head. Maurice on his bed, immersed in his own story. All of us trying our best to ignore the heated, ugly shouts in the next room. I began to read out loud, letting the chant of the adamantine words on the page rise into the air and block the ugliness that was seeping through our wall.

TWO LINES FROM THE BOOK ESPECIALLY SPOKE TO ME: "Janie saw her life like a great tree in leaf with the things suffered, things enjoyed, things done and undone. Dawn and doom was in the branches." I read this to mean that even when the story is painful, the telling of it opens us to a level of vulnerability. What follows is a kind of acceptance, a profoundly beautiful acceptance, of human experience. This was the moment when I knew that Hurston's story had changed me as much as the birth of my baby brother had done. I was inspired to think about my own tree. To consider all my leaves of joy and sadness—the things that made me feel ashamed and insignificant, the things that made me feel proud and strong—and give them their own place on the branches.

I read it again, just so we could all hear the words out loud.

"Dawn and doom was in the branches."

I thought of my father. How he had been both my dawn and my doom. My mother, as well, the way she had once been, cuddled up with me on the beanbag, singing out the syllables as she introduced me to a brand-new word. The way she was now, trapped in a marriage that brought out the worst in her, made her stiff-necked and dissatisfied and snappish, miserable in her discontent. I thought of my younger brothers, too small to remember our lives being anything other than what they were now, but with an entire lifetime ahead of them.

I thought of Ida and Selma—my best friends—as we danced together in their living room. Our shoulders, hips, and heads rolling in sync. The music pushing through us. The way we lifted our faces toward the ceiling in unison, eyes and cheeks shining, buoyed by one another's bliss.

IN 1993, PRESIDENT BILL CLINTON ASKED POET MAYA ANGE-lou to write a poem for his inauguration. I was eleven years old when I first heard her booming voice on our small television. We were all fixated as Angelou recited her original poem "On the Pulse of Morning." I was mesmerized with each stanza. She reminded us that every new hour can hold a new chance. Angelou told us to

Give birth again
To the dream

In her navy winter coat and bright red lipstick, Angelou was the second poet in history to read a poem at a presidential inauguration, a powerful Black woman capturing the attention of the nation. Something in her voice felt familiar, drawing me completely into a new world. Her performance at Clinton's inauguration led to me reading her 1969 autobiography, *I Know Why the Caged Bird Sings*, over and over again. Her prose became like scripture, guiding me through my teenage years. What made a caged bird sing? How did you create a better life for yourself? In a 1977 interview with Jeffrey M. Elliot, Angelou answered my question:

If life teaches us anything, it may be that it's necessary to suffer some defeats. . . . One must learn to care for oneself first, so that one can then dare to care for someone else. That's what it takes to make the caged bird sing.

My reverence for Angelou's poetry introduced me to the renowned poet Paul Laurence Dunbar. The final line of Dunbar's poem "Sympathy" inspired the title of her bestselling book:

I know why the caged bird sings, ah me,
When his wing is bruised and his bosom sore,—

When he beats his bars and he would be free;
It is not a carol of joy or glee,
   But a prayer that he sends from his heart's deep core,
But a plea, that upward to Heaven he flings
I know why the caged bird sings!

Dunbar, a poet born more than a half century before Angelou, masterfully shows us the parallels between life as a Black person and the life of a caged bird. Throughout the poem, the bird yearns for freedom but fails to take flight. Instead, the bird's beautiful song ascends upward to Heaven. I was floored by the poetic connection between Angelou and Dunbar. Their artistry is part of the same lineage and continuous struggle for Black freedom. In her book, Angelou further builds upon Dunbar's eloquent allegory stating: "A bird doesn't sing because it has an answer, it sings because it has a song."

The metaphor was abundantly clear, we all need a story to survive. Soon I would encounter her poem "Weekend Glory." I was attracted to the title for obvious reasons; I pretended it was exclusively for me. This joyful poem by Maya Angelou resonates with strength; I picture a hardworking Black woman, a woman who refuses to conform to the traditional standards of society. Her words provided a much-needed escape. My mother was still working long night shifts and sleeping most of the time she was home. I was still expected to care for my brothers. Money was tight. My father was still gone, leaving me feeling untethered and unsafe. My stepfather continued to crouch in the corner of our home, waging his campaign of sneers and hisses. He continued to make me feel small and ugly and unimportant, to forcibly suppress my voice and demand my silence, obedience, and docility.

Angelou wrote: "Turn away from worry, with a sassy glance." Those words were my first peek into the sense of unbridled joy that Angelou so often brought to her work. Since my father left, my normally sunny and inquisitive nature had dampened and curdled. Joy was not something I often felt in my day-to-day life. Weighed down with the burden of our care and the unhappiness of her marriage, it seemed to me that my mother worked and worked but never stopped worrying. My brothers and I spent most of our time trying to avoid her husband's corrections and punishments. There were no sassy glances in our household. But Angelou's writing showed me that maybe there should be.

As was my habit, I started exploring her other work. Picking up her books, reading just about anything about her that I could find. Many adults are probably familiar with one of Angelou's most famous poems, "Still I Rise," but imagine being an eleven-year-old Black girl, just starting to become aware of our society's limited beauty standards and wondering whether or not I held up to them. Imagine being a pubescent child suffering under the eye of a stepfather who made it his personal quest to make sure I was thoroughly ashamed of my own body and its nascent sexuality. And then imagine me encountering that poem for the first time. The shock and thrill and power of a line like: *Does my sexiness upset you?*

"Still I Rise" was one of the first poems I ever committed entirely to memory. Reciting those lines made me feel wiser than my years. Stronger, safer, more protected. As if I was taking notes on my impending womanhood. I found a deep and restorative connection to Angelou's words. A mixture of elevation, excitement, and relief in the vulnerability on the page. As a writer she instinctively understood the need for words to help process joy, grief, acceptance, and uncertainty.

Angelou's words felt like a powerful secret that could, at least momentarily, protect me from despair whenever I needed them. When things got tough, I held them like a talisman, whispering,

> *Phenomenal woman,*
> *That's me.*

And they worked like a magic spell meant to keep me from harm.

In the essay collection *Wouldn't Take Nothing for My Journey Now,* Angelou writes, "A person is the product of their dreams. So make sure to dream great dreams. And then try to live your dream." That reminded me of something that I had always loved about my father, a quality that I knew he had passed down to me, this spirit of *trying*. This idea that we can't just accept our unhappiness. That we might not always succeed, but we always had to continue moving toward something better. Lost amid the gloom of our shattered family, it was something I had forgotten about myself. Angelou's words felt like a micro-map that led me back to the person I had once been. She showed me the hidden path that could direct me out of the morass of our unhappy household.

She showed me how to find inspiration in the most ordinary experiences, to feel the incredible power of Black history and literature and start to understand its ability to disturb and move society, and then to apply that knowledge to my own personal situation. She encouraged me to keep my heart open and my head up and continue to dream, despite the unbearable circumstances I felt I was living in.

SO ALL OF THIS IS TO SAY THAT, FOUR YEARS LATER, WHEN I received the course list for my senior-year AP English class and saw that we would be reading *I Know Why the Caged Bird Sings*, I was more than a little bit thrilled.

Maya. It felt almost as if we would be studying the words of my wise and favorite auntie, someone I already knew and fiercely loved in a personal way. I had read *Caged Bird* over and over at that point, using Angelou's words to learn how to withstand even the very hardest things with grace and dignity and humor. Hers was the voice that had got me through.

Mr. Burns was my teacher that year. And he was the kind of teacher that most of us are lucky to get once in a lifetime. He was fairly young, with kind eyes and receding sandy-red hair. He loved literature and he loved teaching and he inspired the kind of dedication in his students that made us hang on his every word and accept his opinions as nothing short of brilliant wisdom.

I felt an immediate connection to him, for the work he assigned and his enthusiasm for the texts he was teaching us, the infectious way he shared information, and the fact that he made me feel respected and listened to. He walked that fine balance between encouragement and critical analysis. He made me stretch and work harder than I might have ever done otherwise. As I prepared to finish up high school and move away from Arlington for college, as I tried to imagine what my life would look like outside of this town and the tiny apartment I had been trapped inside for so long, Mr. Burns's class felt like it might be my launching pad, the place where I would find the foundation to support me away from my home.

But as I looked over the rest of our reading list, I felt a little pang of unease. Every year I wondered how my English class syllabus was constructed. It seemed to me like a kind of contract, a promise from teacher to student: Here are all the important things for you to learn in order to pass the test and subsequently cultivate a healthy sense of self.

Yet the books on my reading list told me that some stories are more important than others. Slave narratives were an occasional but resounding yes. Everything else I yearned for—an array of Black fiction, poetry, essays, and memoirs— well, that was glaringly absent from my coursework. Instinctually, I felt a certain kind of rebellion when I failed to see stories that reflected Black history. So, yes! Maya Angelou! And Frederick Douglass was there, too, but beyond that? *To Kill a Mockingbird. Nineteen Eighty-Four.* Ernest Hemingway, William Faulkner, James Joyce, and (I rolled my eyes) the ever-present *Catcher in the Rye.*

I hate *Catcher in the Rye.*

There, I've said it.

And I say this from the point of view of someone who has come back to it again and again over the years, as I've become more objective about craft and how people put together stories, and I've learned to look for other ways to approach and understand the essence of a book. But no matter how many times I've tried, I can't seem to care about a rich, spoiled, rude, misogynistic schoolboy.

For years now, thousands of American high school teachers have presented *Catcher in the Rye* as some sort of sacred offering to their teenage students. A way of saying, "See! I get it! I understand you and all the things you're going through! Here is a mirror of your tortured teenage soul!"

But I never saw anything close to Holden Caulfield when I looked into my mirror. I didn't recognize anything of myself in him. That boy *fenced*, for God's sake! And I couldn't help but feel that all his whining and ennui was unearned and ridiculous. What did he know about pain or survival or loss? What was the point in spending time with this mean and small-souled character?

Still, I trusted Mr. Burns. So I stuffed down my distaste for Salinger and took the test and wrote my paper and was relieved when we got to *Narrative of the Life of Frederick Douglass, an American Slave. Written by Himself.*

Narrative was published in 1845, the first of Douglass's three autobiographies, and is likely the most famous American slave narrative ever published. It is required reading in a majority of high schools, including mine, Wakefield High.

I found this book both brilliant and captivating, but there was something in the way that Mr. Burns approached the study of it that didn't feel quite right. Here, at last, was someone who might be recognizable in my own mirror—or at least in a family photo—but, unlike Holden Caufield, we weren't being asked to see ourselves reflected in this man. We were studying this book like a dry history lesson. It was presented only as a slave narrative, an in-depth examination of the abolitionist movement. And, of course, it *was* those things, but I wished for something more personal.

I was struck by the opening sentence: "I never saw my mother, to know her as such, more than four or five times in my life; and each of these times was very short in duration, and at night."

It seemed that we all longed for our mothers. I imagined Douglass's mother as someone with stately grace and dignity, a figure who would catch the eye in any assembly. In my young mind he had inherited her captivating eyes and thick, coarse hair. Perhaps she was quick-witted and loved to laugh out loud. I determined that she had to be all these things and more. Who else could give birth to such a momentous individual?

I found myself dwelling on one question as we read: How did those who were enslaved ever find anything joyful in their lives? This was something I couldn't bring myself to ask Mr. Burns. It felt ridiculous to consider Black joy when the serious tenets of the abolitionist movement were being discussed in class. Yet I yearned for the simple story of a boy without his mother. And I couldn't help but feel that she deserved at least as much recognition as Douglass's first "owner," Colonel Lloyd, a figure we discussed at length.

I didn't yet have the language to describe the disconnect

I was feeling. Even at my extremely diverse and progressive high school, we never discussed literary representation or delved into the different ways that a book could be othered and how that othering might make a student like me feel alienated and less than seen.

Wakefield High, and Arlington in general, was seen as a community that embodied diversity. There were families of every background, skin color, and nationality in our town, and we were taught from a very young age to be proud of what we considered our almost utopian level of inclusiveness. If someone had asked me, at age eighteen, whether I had ever experienced racism, under the bubble of our forward-thinking community, I would have proudly said no, not ever.

And in many ways, that was true; I had never been called derogatory names or felt personally endangered based on my race. The burden of overt and violent racism was not something I had to contend with. But in other ways, I look back and shake my head at my naïveté and unwillingness to see what was just below the surface.

Years later, after I reconnected with my father, I asked him why he left. And he explained to me that when he had come to the United States, he had been full of ambition and promise. He had expected that if he worked hard, he would be allowed unlimited success in his chosen profession. But instead, as a Black man in America, he was passed up for opportunities and blocked at every turn. He told me that he believed he had no choice but to return to Nigeria, because at least there he could succeed. He could do well enough to build something he could leave behind for Maurice and me.

I lost my father because of racism. But that was also something I couldn't yet recognize or name.

AT LAST, TOWARD THE END OF THE SCHOOL YEAR, WE FI-
nally arrived at what I had been waiting for: Maya Angelou's *I Know Why the Caged Bird Sings.*

I walked into class feeling good. As I took my seat, I
imagined how impressed Mr. Burns would be when he realized that I was already an expert on this particular book. I
was so excited to delve into it in a more structured way. I
couldn't wait to hear what my classmates, and of course Mr.
Burns himself, thought about it. I was certain that he would
love it as much as I did.

"So," said Mr. Burns. He held up a copy of the book and
smiled. "There are a lot of things to admire about this book,
but I think we could all agree that Maya Angelou's grammar
is not one of them."

I don't think I heard a word he said after that. I was gen-
uinely stunned. Of all the things he could have said to intro-
duce this powerful, magnificent book, all the shocking and
difficult and wonderful topics she examined, all the personal
and painful and beautiful truths she had put on the page, *this*
was the way my teacher introduced her to our class?

I knew Angelou's work was steeped in the African
American oral tradition, and I found her prose mesmerizing.
I was absolutely certain that every word, every sentence, the
cadence and rhythm of her work, had been weighed and
considered and deliberately chosen. I believed her to be a genius way beyond someone like Salinger—and certainly at

least on par with anyone else we had studied that year. And I couldn't believe that Mr. Burns would so casually dismiss her talent and craftmanship, make her seem small and ignorant.

Outside of *Narrative,* Angelou's book was the only other autobiography I had ever read by a Black person. A Black woman, no less.

I envy anyone who has yet to read *I Know Why the Caged Bird Sings*. I will never forget my first reading of it, how my mind raced with visions of Angelou, and the warm sensation that I felt throughout my body. Instinctively, my entire being recognized I was encountering something special. Maya Angelou's autobiography has been part of my interior world since I first picked it up in middle school. My copy has grown tattered, the front cover ripped, and the pages faded to a yellowish hue. The margins are filled with the incoherent musings of my younger self. My favorite observation is lightly scratched in pencil at the beginning of chapter 23. It reads, "Graduations mark a new beginning." In this chapter Maya, at that time, known as Marguerite, is graduating from the eighth grade. She is radiant and beaming in a yellow dress. She writes "My dress fitted perfectly and everyone said that I looked like a sunbeam in it." At my own eighth-grade graduation, I felt that same glow, a sense of pride and anticipation. I was entering high school and inching closer to adulthood. From the seventh grade onward, her writing meant everything to me. Even beyond her poetry, this memoir had made me feel as if I knew her with an intimacy to which I shouldn't have been privy. She was comfort. She gave me pride in being a young, ambitious woman—and in being a woman of African descent. She would eventually lead me to Nikki Giovanni and James Baldwin and Ntozake Shange and Toni Morrison, and to my own career as a writer. Because, as Maya Angelou showed me, a Black girl *could* be a writer. And that same Black girl could write her own authentic experience in her own voice.

The first time I read *Caged Bird* I couldn't articulate what moved me, but I knew there was something, some truth telling, on those pages that—in my mind, at least—Black people weren't supposed to say in public. Who, from my neighborhood, for instance, would admit to any kind of family dysfunction? Who would admit to not having certain clothes? Enough food? Who talked about sex? Who talked about sexual assault? Who talked about desire or even love?

Certainly not me. I held our family secrets as close as I could. But Angelou showed me that if I gained the courage, there could be another way.

The prose struck me as a familiar way of speaking that had suddenly become eloquent. It was like how people talked at home—if they would talk this openly—but the way it was presented made it sound elevated. The language of my life suddenly felt like high art.

And then, in one offhand remark, Mr. Burns made the language of my life feel like it was an ignorant mistake. The fact that Mr. Burns was somehow invalidating Maya Angelou's voice felt like he was invalidating me as well.

———

I LEFT THAT CLASS FEELING FURIOUS AND HURT. I HAD waded through an entire year of white, male "classics" waiting for my chance to feel like I was truly included in the conversation, but now that we had arrived, it was as if I had been told that because we were not speaking in traditional, proper English, the discussion wasn't even really worth having.

Maybe it wouldn't have mattered if I hadn't loved or respected Mr. Burns so much. If he had been the kind of teacher I generally disagreed with, or disliked, I would have just dismissed the insult and ignorance and moved on. But I actively cared about what Mr. Burns thought, and his critique of this book that had meant so much to me felt like nothing less than a slap in my face.

I ranted to Ida and Selma during lunch. "I mean, what does he know? Who gets to make these rules, anyway?" I wanted to protest, to complain, but I didn't know what adult I could possibly talk to who might actually vouch for how wrong this all felt.

And honestly, even if I did have an adult I could talk to about it, I wasn't entirely sure how to explain what was so wrong with what had been said. I didn't have the language or literary sophistication to unpack my anger or sense of being dismissed. I didn't have any Black teachers. I didn't have supplemental or critical material being given to me. There was no Google yet. I only knew that what Mr. Burns had said felt like a violation, but I wasn't exactly sure how to express why.

Still, I came to class the next day ready to battle. I had stayed up almost all night, nursing my sense of outrage and arguing with the Mr. Burns in my head.

I passed him at his desk, pointedly refusing to return his smile as I made my way to my seat. I impatiently waited for him to take roll call, and then I raised my hand.

"Yes, Glory?"

"Mr. Burns, I want to talk about the fact that you dismissed Maya Angelou's ability as a writer yesterday." (I had scripted this careful opening salvo in my head the night before.)

Mr. Burns raised his eyebrows. "And how did I do that?"

"You said that her grammar was not correct."

The other kids in class perked up and started watching us like we were a tennis match, whipping their heads back and forth between us as we spoke.

Mr. Burns's mouth quirked up at one corner. "Ah. I see. I don't think that I entirely dismissed her as a writer by saying that, but you must admit that her grammar is often glaringly wrong."

I shook my head. "I think she did that on purpose. I think maybe she did that so that her characters . . . sounded right."

"What could be right about sloppy grammar?"

I felt my face heat up. "I don't think you understand her. I feel like you're missing the point of what she was trying to do. And I guess I don't understand why you even assigned this book if you were just going to insult it."

"This is not the first text I've assigned and then critiqued, Glory." He said this mildly.

I knew that was true. Mr. Burns made a point of talking about the weaknesses and strengths of all the books we read, and he always encouraged us to do the same. But this was different. The other writers he had critiqued had not been

Black. And the language they had used had not been solely *my* language, Black vernacular English.

But I didn't say this. I didn't know if I was even allowed to say this. "It just didn't feel good. What you said."

He sat down on the edge of his desk. "I am more than happy to have this discussion with you. I'm very glad you brought it up, but if you are going to challenge me on this, you need to be able to tell me more than what you 'feel.' It can't just be an emotional response."

I bit my lip. I was eighteen. Everything was a little bit emotional to me in those days. And now, when I look back on that discussion, especially after having worked with so many young people, I feel like an emotional response to something should never be ignored or taken as without value. Because that emotional response is the way you learn to trust your own intuition. It's the way you build your sense of innately knowing that something is not right.

We continued our discussion. Mr. Burns patiently listening, then poking and prodding at me, encouraging me to try to find the words to express exactly why I was so upset, and why I felt he was so very wrong.

As the discussion progressed (and other kids must have been included, but in my memory it was solely a conversation between Mr. Burns and me), I felt a heady rush of freedom. There was a sense of liberation in even being allowed to have this conversation. At home, with my mother, simply asking a question was viewed as disrespecting my elders. I was constantly told what to do but never asked for my opinion on anything. And I was certainly never encouraged to argue with any adults I knew. But here was Mr. Burns, inviting my thoughts, listening carefully to my words, trying to help me figure out how to make my argument. Even if he didn't entirely agree with me, I think I did change his mind a little bit. Or maybe I gave him something to think about. And at the very least, he was treating me with the kind of respect and consideration that I hadn't felt from an adult since I had lost my father. Even as I get older and gain wisdom and understand things that I simply didn't at eighteen, I sometimes find myself still arguing with Mr. Burns in my head.

That argument sharpened me a little for what was to come. My beloved teacher's failure to recognize Maya Angelou's undeniable genius gave me a brief and vivid peek into the literary biases I would come up against again and again. It showed me that not all adults, even the smart ones, were right all the time—and that it was actually okay to challenge them. It made it very clear that even the most sincere, well-meaning, supposedly enlightened person could have blind spots and insensitivities. That people I loved and respected (most especially white people) would sometimes speak carelessly and wound me without meaning to, and I would then have to decide whether to confront them or let their ignorance pass through me. And that sometimes, when I did decide to confront them, it could breed the kind of discussion that I had with Mr. Burns, one where I actually ended up feeling heard and understood rather than being dismissed and made small.

I was proud of myself at the end of that day. And I'm pretty sure Mr. Burns was proud of me, too.

YEARS LATER, WHEN I WAS ATTENDING HOWARD UNIVER-
sity, Maya Angelou came to campus, and I had the honor
of asking her to sign one of her books. It was a collection
of her poetry, including "Weekend Glory," and as I stood
before her, I wanted to blurt out everything she meant to
me. Everything she had done for me and taught me. The
way she showed me how to romanticize my life. The way
she had reminded me to value *trying*. How she taught me
that telling my truth was the only way toward happiness.
How she had encouraged me to be gentle with myself, and
create tender moments, and be kind to myself even when—
or actually, *especially* when—no one else was showing me
kindness. How she had shown me that I could do anything, *be* anything. That it was all within the realm of my
possibility.

But instead, I handed her the book and told her my name.
She met my eyes and smiled that gorgeous smile of hers and
repeated my name back to me in that unmistakable con-
tralto, and then bent her head to write.

I walked away from her, out of the building and into the
crisp autumn air, before I reopened the cover to read what
she had written.

For Glory Edim.
Joy!
Maya Angelou

Mr. Burns had a tradition, which I imagine he might
keep up even to this very day, that on the last day of AP En-

glish, each of his senior students received both a letter and a poem that he had written for us.

This was the first stanza of mine:

Your day has the purpose of morning.
Stop right there. Throw your head back—breathe it in
    wait an extra moment to exhale.
Photograph it as it unfolds, dare to develop, frame it for
    posterity, hang it above your head, your heart.
When you reach for it, no matter how blindly, it will be there,
    hanging.
When people ask, be sure to tell the story.

I read those lines from my teacher and I laughed. As it turned out, Mr. Burns and Maya Angelou had something in common. Despite the limitations of his class, or the fact that I sometimes craved more than he was capable of giving me, this teacher had made me feel valued. He made me feel seen. At a time when all the other important adults in my life belittled and dismissed me, and wanted me to be less than I was, when there were so many narrow spaces in my life, Mr. Burns had created enough room and safety for me to be my full and authentic self.

In this way, Mr. Burns and Maya Angelou were the same. They offered me a mirror. They believed in me. They knew I was capable of greatness. They showed me that I was valuable and lovable and had the greatest kind of worth.

They both gave me permission to tell my story. They both gave me joy.

CHAPTER FOUR

Alice Walker, *In Search of Our Mothers' Gardens*; Margaret Walker, "For My People"; bell hooks, *Ain't I a Woman: Black Women and Feminism*; Maya Angelou; Kahlil Gibran

In the early fall of my senior year of high school, my whole world seemed to revolve around the SATs. Now that I'm an adult, I look back and think, *Why was I so nervous?* But at the time, it seemed like there would be no future for me at all if I didn't earn the proper score on that test. I had worked so hard to get good grades, taken full advantage of the great schools and endless extracurriculars my mother had insisted on, but the SATs felt like the final thing standing in the way of me getting into the college of my choice and finally being able to leave Arlington and get on with the rest of my life.

I'd taken the test at the end of the summer, and the results were excruciatingly slow to arrive. I was fairly certain that I had done well on the English portion, but I had always been terrible at math, and I worried that my math score would be so low that it would tank the whole test. Every day

I would rush home, looking for that envelope in the mail, and every day I would be disappointed. I could hardly think of anything else. I was obsessed.

So when I walked out of school and saw the Mercury Topaz parked there with my mom waving at me from behind the wheel, I immediately knew why she was there.

I slid into the passenger seat, and she held up an envelope.

"It's here," she said.

I felt my heart contract as I reached toward her, but my mom quickly pulled the envelope out of my reach and met my eyes.

"Whatever it is, it will be fine." Her voice was calm and reassuring. "You've got this. You have worked very hard, and even if you're not happy, you can always take it again if you need to."

I nodded, my mouth too dry to answer, and started to reach again, but my mother shook her head. "First, we're going to have a treat," she said firmly.

She put the envelope into her pocket, then put the car into gear.

We drove to a nearby Roy Rogers, and I forced myself to act like I was hungry as my mother hovered behind me, insisting that I take advantage of the restaurant's policy of letting the customer do all the fixings themselves.

"Make sure you get extra pickles!" she commanded as I loaded up my burger. "That slice of tomato looks good. No, not that one! The one behind it. Do you want extra fries?"

She wanted me fed and well. But she also knew how anxious I was. She knew that I thought my entire future would hinge on this score. So she accepted it when I finally admitted that I was too nervous to eat, and she directed me back into the car.

"Now?" I asked.

She shook her head. "Not yet."

And off we went, driving around Arlington, taking the long way home. She just kept talking and talking to me, commenting on the scenery as we drove by, chattering about my brothers, wondering what the weather would be like tomorrow, just casually doing her best to try to get me to relax.

We finally parked outside of our apartment complex, and she took the envelope out of her pocket and handed it over.

"Okay. Now you can open it."

I don't remember my actual score, but I do remember screaming, "I'M GOING TO COLLEGE!" and my mother laughing and reaching past the steering wheel to hug me, and then turning on the radio, and finding the local radio station, 93.9, which she never played because she preferred to listen to classical or church music. She played it super loud as we jumped around in our seats and hollered and celebrated, and then she turned the music off, and she bent her head and prayed, giving thanks, and then she smiled and hugged me one more time, and then I got out of the car and watched her drive off, back to work the night shift at the hospital.

THE WOMAN BEHIND THE COUNTER HANDED ME BACK THE piece of paper and I squeezed my eyes shut in despair. It was unbelievable. I had failed the test to get my driver's permit.

For the tenth time.

It made absolutely no sense. It was a simple written test. I didn't even have to get behind the wheel. Most sixteen-year-olds passed this thing on their first try. And here I was, a college freshman, a person who had always been a wiz at exams, getting my tenth notice of failure.

My friends laughed when I told them. "Girl, what is wrong with you?" they asked, shaking their heads.

"Who cares, anyway," I muttered as I stomped out of the cafeteria, too mad to eat. "I don't even like cars."

That, of course, was an outright lie. Maybe I wasn't allowed to drive one, but I loved cars. I loved the Grand Cherokee that my high school boyfriend L had faithfully chauffeured me around in. I loved the two-door silver Honda Civic that Ida and Selma raced through the back streets behind our apartment complex. And more than anything, I loved the old cream-colored Mercury Topaz that my mother had driven for most of my life.

AFTER HIGH SCHOOL, I'D LEFT ARLINGTON IN A RUSH, ready to be away from my abusive stepfather, the responsibility of caring for my brothers, my mother's watchful eye, and what felt like her constant criticism. I was young and self-involved and often felt sorry for myself; I kept comparing my life to the experiences of my peers, who seemed to be better off. They had more access to material things: bigger houses, longer dining room tables, vacations on an airplane and not in their cars. My heart still harbored a jagged and painful wound where my father had once been, and in my naïveté, I felt that these superficial amenities would somehow fill that hole, and that their lack in my life proved just how little my mother cared.

When I left for college, I told myself that I was glad to leave home, glad to leave my family—and most especially my mother—behind. I was ready to reinvent myself, to figure out who I really was and what I wanted. I imagined that the key to that reinvention was discarding what felt like my unhappy past. I decided that I wouldn't miss my mother at all, that I would hardly spare her a thought.

But then I was assigned Alice Walker's *In Search of Our Mothers' Gardens,* and Margaret Walker's poem "For My People," and bell hooks's essay *Ain't I a Woman: Black Women and Feminism.* After tearing through those words in great, rapacious gulps, I emerged, gasping for breath, with nothing but my mother on my mind.

IN ALICE WALKER'S *IN SEARCH OF OUR MOTHERS' GARDENS,* IT seemed that Walker was always in her car, on the road to somewhere: protests or teaching jobs or, in her most famous piece, to find Zora Neale Hurston's unmarked grave. It made me think of my mother's figurative drive for independence, and how she literally expressed that independence through her old, beat-up used car. I read Walker's thoughts on Black feminism and Black ideas about how women could assert themselves, and I thought of my mother trying to make her way out of no way, how she was constantly searching for spaces where she wouldn't be limited by her circumstances.

My mother learned to drive as a young woman in Nigeria, but she had to relearn from scratch when she immigrated to the United States to marry my father. Driving in Nigeria was totally different than driving in the United States. In Nigeria you drove using mainly intuition and suggestion. The roads were mostly dirt, there were very few stop signs and even fewer traffic lights, and you could pick and choose what rules you felt needed to be followed at any given time. When my mom first got on the road in Virginia, she felt accosted by all the stop signs and red lights and green and blue traffic signs dictating the law. She complained that she couldn't pay attention to the actual driving because she was always trying to remember the endless rules of those American roads.

Still, she was determined to figure it out and get it right. For my mother, who had left behind her country and her family and her job as a teacher to marry a man she barely knew and stay at home to raise their children, driving meant some of the only independence she had left. She was not willing to lose her ability to take herself from place to place.

My mother was most terrified of the heavy traffic and fast speed on highways, but around Arlington they could not be avoided. So she would wait until late at night—when the roads were almost empty and my father, brother, and I peacefully slept—and leave the house to speed up and down Route 66, endlessly practicing until she felt she was competent enough to safely ferry me and Maurice around.

Before my father left, I had plenty of time with my mother. My father's job and paycheck allowed her to be home with us, to cook our meals and help me with my homework, to read to me and tuck me into bed every night. The drives we took with her back then were just short jaunts to the supermarket, or maybe to church—necessary everyday excursions. But after my father left, my mother had to support us on her own. That meant night shifts and double shifts, picking up extra work whenever she could, and sleeping for most of the day so that she had the energy to get up and do it all over again. This is when the car, and our drives together, became something else, something much more important.

IN HER ESSAY *AIN'T I A WOMAN: BLACK WOMEN AND FEMINISM,* bell hooks wrote about how the key to women's liberation, according to white feminism, was the right to work. White feminists were all about their right to leave their identities as housewives and helpmates behind and get equal access to the fruits of the white patriarchy.

This was a laughable concept when applied to someone like my mother and to the masses of American women who already worked—not for self-actualization, but out of necessity. For them, work didn't lead to liberation. It didn't allow them to gain economic success. It was just what they did to survive. They were seen as units of labor who lived from paycheck to meager paycheck, working as hard and long as they possibly could. They worked, but instead of finding this oft-promised satisfaction and self-worth, they were left exhausted and spent, robbed of any real time to spend with their families, or even to have a private thought to themselves.

Because of this, after my father left, the car became the only place where I could regain what had once been my mother's undivided attention. We didn't have the time or opportunity to have the kind of nightly meals at the dinner table that all the parenting books insisted every functional family needed. But in between her shifts at work, my mother drove us places.

She was reaching for her own American dream, and my mother's plan of action was to achieve it by creating opportunities for my brothers and me. She made sure that we went to great schools, and she signed us up for every possible extracurricular opportunity. In between work shifts, she dropped us off at baseball games and cheerleading practice and SAT prep. I went to Brownies and ballet. Maurice attended a Spanish immersion class. She delivered us right up to the doors of each opportunity, but she could never take the time to park and walk through with us to enjoy any of it. She would sit in the car for a moment, engine still running, waiting for us to safely pass through, and then put the car into gear and drive right back to work.

Traveling from one destination to the other was the only free time my mother seemed to have for us, so the Mercury Topaz quickly became the space where the biggest moments of our lives took place. When it was time to celebrate, my mom would take us in the car. When we were getting punished, my mom would also throw us into the car. Any long talks or important announcements—they happened in that car.

———

THERE IS AN INTERVIEW THAT MAYA ANGELOU DID IN THE late 1970s that resulted in one of my all-time favorite quotations: "Each of us has that right, that possibility, to invent ourselves daily. If a person does not invent herself, she will be invented." And in so many ways, every time my mom left the house, when she got into that car to drive herself to work, she invented herself on the way. She put aside her exhaustion and worry and disappointment. She straightened her shoulders and took a deep breath and became someone who did what she had to do to give us a future.

I remember sitting in my dorm room, reading Kahlil Gibran's poem "On Work." When I came to the line "Work is love made visible," I stopped reading and rocked back in my seat, recognizing something that I hadn't been wise enough to see up until that moment.

I LOVED WATCHING MY MOTHER DRIVE ALMOST AS MUCH as she loved driving. She had this intense focus, this clarity about her. When she was behind the wheel, there was a glimmer and shine to her—she came alive. My mom has always been a beautiful woman. But she isn't only physically beautiful; she has a presence about her. And when I read Alice and Margaret and bell and Maya, I recognized that same kind of presence in these brilliant Black feminists. And though my mom probably wouldn't have called herself a feminist, or ever use words like *patriarchy* or *male domination* or *sexism*, I realized that she embodied that same brilliance and strength that these writers had. She was so brave and bold in circumstances that didn't favor her.

In the years leading up to my birth, a cohort of prolific Black women writers published books and changed the literary landscape. In 1970, writer Toni Cade Bambara was determined to curate a collection of literature by, for, and about Black women. She gathered an exceptional group of scholars and artists, including Adele Jones and Francee Covington; actresses Abbey Lincoln and Verta Mae Smart-Grosvenor; authors Nikki Giovanni, Alice Walker, and Audre Lorde— inviting them to share their unique perspectives on Black womanhood. The result was a groundbreaking anthology entitled *The Black Woman* that centered Black feminism, motherhood, and liberation politics.

The Bluest Eye, the first novel written by Toni Morrison, was also published in 1970. The book's protagonist, Pecola Breedlove, believes that if her eyes were blue, she would then finally be beautiful. The novel was a doorway for every Black girl yearning to define herself amid unattainable ideals of beauty centered on whiteness. Morrison dared to explore identity in a way that was unspoken and painful for Black women. Generations of Black women immediately recognized themselves in Pecola's longing. After I finished reading *The Bluest Eye*, I wept. Pecola Breedlove's yearning for blue eyes devastated me. I began to see my world, as Pecola did, filled with half-truths and harsh judgments.

BOOK BY BOOK, WE WITNESSED OUR INTIMATE LIVES AND everyday fears being acknowledged on the page. *for colored girls who have considered suicide / when the rainbow is enuf* by Ntozake Shange was published in 1976. Alice Walker's *The*

Color Purple and *You Can't Keep a Good Woman Down* were published in 1982, along with Audre Lorde's *Zami*. Followed by Paule Marshall's *Praisesong for the Widow* in 1983. The brilliance would continue steadily for decades, with Black women writers winning accolades and capturing our literary imagination. Walker's *The Color Purple* became the first work by a Black woman to win the Pulitzer Prize for Fiction. In 1988, Morrison would go on to win a Pulitzer Prize and an American Book Award for *Beloved*. As I grew into adulthood, so did the literary canon. Their books lined my bookshelves and defined a cohort of exceptional contemporary Black women writers. Their words were elegant, powerful, and satisfyingly potent; I never completed a book without a renewed sense of possibility. Between 1970 and 1989, Black women were not only being published, they were finally being understood. All monumental narratives written exclusively by and for Black women.

When I read Margaret Walker's poem "Lineage," I thought about the reverence that both Margaret and Alice Walker showed for their mothers and grandmothers and their grandmothers' grandmothers: "My grandmothers are full of memories."

I thought about the way that Alice Walker had pushed through a field of thorns and hidden snakes to find Zora Neale Hurston's unmarked grave. I thought about the way these women honored the matriarchs who came before them. And I felt like I had failed to take advantage of the time I'd had with my mother.

I didn't know my own lineage. I didn't know the history or legacy of the women who had come before me. I knew nothing about the matriarchs in my own family. I wondered why I had never asked my mother about her mother and grandmother. I realized I had been too self-involved, not curious enough. I realized that if I didn't know the women who came before me, I wouldn't have a chance of figuring out who I was meant to be.

I made a vow to myself that the next time I was home, the next time we were riding around in the car, I would make sure that I asked my mother all the right questions. I would do my own anthropological study on the women in my family, starting with my mother. I wouldn't let the moment pass.

But, as it turned out, it would be years before I had that chance again.

AS I WRITE THESE WORDS, I STILL DON'T HAVE MY DRIVER'S license. I did, on my eleventh try, eventually pass the written test, but then I moved to New York City, where a driver's license is fairly useless. I learned the subway system and how to hail a cab, and that felt like it was adult and sophisticated enough.

And it turned out that I didn't need a car to find my independence or figure out who I was. That work would be done not behind the wheel but curled up in a cozy spot in my apartment, or as I gently rocked on a train between stops, or in my bed at night, the comforter tucked up at my waist, the pages of my book illuminated by the soft glow of my bedside lamp.

I sometimes think about that string of failed tests at the

DMV. Why I couldn't seem to pass that simple exam. And I wonder if it was because, for so long, being driven around by my boyfriend, my friends, and, most especially, my mother was really the only time when it felt like anyone was truly taking care of me. I cooked and I cleaned and I cared for my brothers. I was a little woman for so long, starting at so young an age. Of course I would have this resistance to losing my seat in the passenger side of the car. Of course I would cling to this one last place where I could cede control and just let someone else make the decisions and set our path. Maybe I wasn't ready to lose the one small piece of being a beloved and protected child that I had left.

YEARS LATER, WHEN I FIRST FOUND OUT I WAS PREGNANT, I visited two bridges in two days. The pregnancy was a surprise, but one that made me almost instantly dizzy with happiness. The joys of raising my two brothers had always outweighed the hardships, and there had never been a time in my life when I didn't both deeply want and absolutely expect to be a mother.

Still, I needed some time to digest the news before sharing it with my then-partner, so after I took the test at Planned Parenthood, I walked across the Brooklyn Bridge. There were so many things to figure out. My partner and I were living in a tiny studio. My career was taking almost all my time and energy. I ate out for every meal. I traveled all the time. None of my friends were building families yet. We were not that young, but we were all living in the perpetual

Peter Pan state that Brooklyn seems to wrap its denizens in. In some ways, we were all still waiting for our real lives to begin.

And now mine finally was.

But what kind of mother would I be? I wondered. I thought of Ms. Doris, my friend Petrushka's mother. She was the kind of mom who not only seemed to know everything about her daughter—her biggest dreams, her secret crushes, her favorite color—but also knew those things about her daughter's friends. She taught us how to pray together. She gave me my first office job. It felt like she had so much extra attention and time to give, it even spilled out over me. Because if I meant something to her daughter, I meant something to her as well.

My mother could not have said what my favorite color was, or even understood why there would be any need to know that information.

Perhaps Ms. Doris had more time and fewer demons than my mother did. I don't think she had to worry so much about the fundamentals of survival—food, rent, avoiding deportation—like my mother did. I didn't fully know what burdened her. But I realize Ms. Doris had the ability and perhaps the luxury of being present in my life. And for that I am forever grateful.

YOU ARE NOT YOUR MOTHER, I TOLD MYSELF AS I WALKED across the bridge, gingerly touching my belly. *You are not scraping for survival. You have resources. You have support. You will have time. You have the ability to parent this child. You're not a teenager. You're not some girl, about to go off to college and start your life. You're an adult. You can do this.*

The next day I flew to San Francisco for work. Though I was certain I would keep this baby, I still hadn't told my partner. I wanted the weekend to think about it. To consider what it would mean. That evening, I made my way to Marshall's Beach and looked up at the Golden Gate Bridge as it stretched out over the water, shining through the fog, from one dark mound of rock to the other.

I took a selfie, aiming down so my still-flat belly was in the photo. Here we were. The first picture of my baby and me.

You will need to learn to drive, I thought.

AND NOW I HAVE A CHILD OF MY OWN, AND I NO LONGER live in New York City, and my partner is my ex-partner, and soon I will take my driver's exam, behind the wheel this time, and I am determined that I will pass that test.

I have more time than my mother did. More money. More support. I don't have to ration out the attention I give my son. He knows that if he talks, I will listen. We chat and snuggle on our couch at home. We have dinner together at the table every night. I bathe him. I read to him in his little bed. I have the immense privilege of being fully present for my child.

But I also want to give him something my mother gave to me. I want to surprise my boy by picking him up from school when he's not expecting me. I want to play his favorite music and sing along with him as we roll through the streets. I still want to have those long, deep conversations that only happen when you sit side by side, watching the scenery as it slides by through a rainy window, not meeting each other's eyes, but somehow exposing your hearts and souls.

I want my chance to take the long way home.

PART II

To tell the truth is to become beautiful, to begin to love yourself, value yourself. And that's political, in its most profound way.

JUNE JORDAN

CHAPTER FIVE

William Shakespeare, *Romeo and Juliet*; Toni Morrison, *Jazz*; bell hooks, *all about love*; Toni Cade Bambara, *The Black Woman: An Anthology*

Sometimes, books were dangerous. Sometimes, they steered me wrong. Sometimes, I would dip in to pages too sophisticated for my young mind and things would fly right over my innocent head. Sometimes, I was not experienced enough to understand the true message an author was trying to convey. Sometimes I would read what I wanted to read, stopping halfway through the beginning of a beautiful sentence, and embrace the fragment, the unfinished words, the incomplete thought, as profound truth. I would shrug off the actual point of things, wandering down a perilous path that the authors were very likely trying to turn me away from. Particularly when it came to love.

GROWING UP, I DIDN'T HAVE MANY—OR REALLY ANY— decent models of successful romantic relationships to look at. There were a few brief, hazy, golden years when my mother and father were still together and looked relatively content to my young eyes. But when I think back on that time, I now wonder just how happy they honestly could have been. They had never even been on a date before they decided to marry. They only spent a year together before they had their first child. They were struggling to get by in a difficult and sometimes hostile country far from their home and culture and extended family.

I suppose that if their marriage had actually survived, instead of crumbling under the weight of my father's infidelities and my mother's disappointments, it would be considered a great love story. I look at a picture of my parents from their traditional wedding in Nigeria, and they are so beautiful. My dad is ridiculously handsome; my mom is stunning. Everyone around them is smiling. The façade is nearly perfect, and their story seems so wildly romantic: Two people who were barely more than strangers clasped hands and took a grand leap into the unknown. If they hadn't ended up hating each other by the end of things, it would have been a miracle of the highest order. For some reason, we always hope that foolish beginnings can resolve themselves into blissful endings.

But obviously, the marriage was in no way blissful, and it did not survive, and my front-row seat to its demise (and later, being witness to my mother's second, even more unhappy, union and eventual divorce) left me with no realistic answer to the question of how to truly love and be loved. It was something I was desperate to learn. In my mind, there was no higher calling or more important puzzle to be solved. I was determined that love—once it came into my life— would be both successful and sustained.

SHAKESPEARE'S *ROMEO AND JULIET* WAS THE FIRST PLACE I looked. Like many adolescent girls of my particular genera- tion, I had been mesmerized by Baz Luhrmann's splashy, sexy film version of the play. To my fifteen-year-old eyes, Leonardo DiCaprio's reed-thin lover boy Romeo and Claire Danes's chin-constantly-jerking-with-uncontainable-emotion Juliet seemed to be the epitome of true love. And the fact that true love ended in tragic death? That just made it all the more desirable to me. Better a dramatic double suicide than the interminable poisonous drip of my parents' resentments and hissed arguments.

Ah, I thought, *here was something I could understand. If you love someone, you sacrifice for them. You martyr yourself to the cause. You give up everything you have—even life itself—in order to deserve their devotion.*

I understood this message because I had been taught to show my love this way for years. I cared for my brothers with exactly this kind of sacrifice in mind. It made sense to me; if you loved someone, their needs must always come be- fore your own. And deep down, I was certain that once I found my Romeo, he would feel the exact same way. We might end up in a bloody, fiery suicide pact, trying to outdo each other in our grand gestures of martyrdom, but dead or alive, our souls would be forever connected.

Of course, as an adult, I look at *Romeo and Juliet* and I think, *How young, how impulsive, how wasteful. Those children didn't know each other at all!* And why did I dismiss Lady Capulet's wisdom? She loved her daughter; she wanted the best for her. Maybe she actually did know what would have made Juliet truly happy. After all, Paris turned out to be Paul Rudd (aka Mr. Perfect), and Romeo ended up with a pussy posse.

I read the play now, and I see the obvious parallel with my own parents' story. I shake my head at how blind I was then. I wish I could slap some sense into my younger self, fervidly admiring the shallow and impulsive lust driving all those bad decisions. Taking it all so literally. Not seeing the play for the warning it truly was.

Why was I so impressed by lines like "Palm to palm is holy palmers kiss," when right from the beginning Shakespeare shouted his real message about love loud and clear? We meet Romeo, claiming his endless love for Rosaline (who shall be forgotten momentarily. How did my fifteen-year-old self miss that particular detail?) almost as prettily as he ever speaks of Juliet, and he says,

> *Love is a smoke raised with a fume of sighs;*
> *Being purged, a fire sparkling in lovers' eyes;*
> *Being vex'd, a sea nourish'd with lovers' tears;*
> *What is it else? a madness most discreet,*
> *a choking gall and a preserving sweet.*

Romeo's view of love was already dysfunctional and twisted. The doom, the tragedy, the waste, the fact that this was all going to go so very wrong, was made clear as day. But teen Glory somehow saw this mess as a map to the stars.

I HAD A STEADY HIGH SCHOOL BOYFRIEND, L. HE WAS HAND-some and sweet and dedicated to me. He drove me and my brothers around whenever we needed a ride. He held my hand and, occasionally, we chastely kissed. He respected my young, faith-driven determination to keep away from temptation and sin. He was good and kind, and what was between us felt innocent and pure. I could have married him. I could have stayed in Arlington and been his wife. We would have moved into a small house or apartment, a starter home. We would have had our children when we were young. We wouldn't have been rich, but probably not so terribly poor, either. We might have been happy.

But we were not Romeo and Juliet. There was no drama, no obsession, no version of our relationship where I could imagine that we ended up draped over each other, cold and pale, lips stained with poison, heart wound dripping with blood, forever entangled. So when the time came for me to leave Arlington and go to college, I kissed L goodbye and silently wondered if what had been between us could be considered real love at all.

MY FIRST YEAR OF COLLEGE WAS NOT WHAT I EXPECTED IT to be. I had decided on Trinity College and I'd entered hopeful and eager, but I almost immediately found myself adrift.

It never occurred to me that college was the place where you took the time to figure out what you actually wanted to be. I thought I had to know what I wanted from the very start, but it simply wasn't clear to me yet, and so I felt panicked, like I was wasting my time. I longed for nothing so much as someone to tell me what to do.

And so, a little bit scared and definitely out of patience, I decided, without my mother's permission or knowledge, to take a semester off. I suspended my enrollment, got a job as a hostess at a popular diner in Adams Morgan, and, while I was waiting to see what would come next, I read *Jazz* by Toni Morrison and *all about love* by bell hooks.

Have there ever been two wiser people than these writers? Both of them shine with brilliance and compassion. Their books are treasure chests, their words are gleaming jewels of creativity, their thoughts are rich and complex and, when studied carefully, can surely light the way through almost any problem.

But there I was again, refusing to see the point.

Morrison's story—about a married man, Joe, who becomes so obsessed with his much-younger lover, Dorcas, that he kills her rather than allowing her to be with anyone else, and the dramatic response of his long-suffering wife, Violet— was surely never meant to be a paragon of romance, but I was absolutely fixated on Morrison's opening scene. There was Violet on her way to cut a dead girl's face. The story continues to unravel from there. Somehow I thought this book the most beautiful, romantic, soul-stirring piece of writing I'd ever read. I thought it absolutely encapsulated what love should be. I thought that Violet doing unspeakable things, like mutilating the dead girl that her husband had loved, and then shoving her pet birds out into the snow, showed just how devoted she was to Joe. I was convinced that death and love and sacrifice were intertwined, and that Morrison was telling me that in order to truly love, you have to reconfigure yourself. You needed to morph into the object of your affection. Lose yourself so you could become something bigger. I thought she was saying that two could become one, and in order to make that happen? You had to give up a piece of your soul.

It should have been the character Dorcas I related to. She was my age and inexperienced like me. She was just starting to test out her world. But it was actually Violet I was drawn toward. It didn't make sense. I wasn't a childless, middle-aged, married woman. Romantic love had not betrayed me yet. No boy had broken my heart.

But, of course, the biggest wound I carried was the loss of my father, and perhaps I related to the pain Violet felt when she almost lost the most important man in her life. And, maybe I thought that if only my mother had been as steadfast as Violet, if only she had forgiven my father's infidelities, had been willing to ignore her own needs, had found a way through, my father might still be in my life.

Violet was who I wanted to be. She was the one who regularly sacrificed to make love stay, and I understood that impulse. I had sacrificed so much in my familial relationships that I believed those kinds of sacrifices would be necessary in my romantic life as well.

As with *Romeo and Juliet,* the carefully crafted beauty of Morrison's words bewitched me, allowing me to blithely ignore the bigger, darker message she was trying to convey. In a novel entitled *Jazz*, you could not miss the literal rhythm of the author's writing. The way her sentences slammed against each other, the lyrical quality in her word choices, the overarching metaphor that compared romance to jazz: unpredictable, improvised, with high and low tempos. The rhythmic beat (be it heart or drum) that continues as long as two people choose to make a life together.

Reading *Jazz* made me want to find and understand my own sound. What was it? What did it mean? How would it sound in chorus with another person? How would it feel to be in love? I was almost certain that true love would sound like death. That's what I thought Shakespeare and Morrison were telling me. I thought you had to kill yourself or be willing to die—or kill—for someone. Death or sacrifice. Either literal or metaphorical. That's how you proved you love somebody.

I was certain—absolutely sure—that this was what Morrison was telling me to do.

And let me be clear—she wasn't. She absolutely was not. She was examining human, romantic love with a keen and clear eye, acting as a witness, using her genius to show just how messed up and confused we can be. How, if we are not careful, our pasts can override our present. How our faulty, foolish hearts can lead us toward all the wrong things. How unthinking passion can trigger all our faults and worst impulses and leave us in a rubble of our own making.

But my younger self blithely cherry-picked words and messages, and willfully ignored Morrison's brilliance and warnings. I decided that I would be a Violet. Or I would be the unnamed narrator who closes the tragic story with the immolating desire of these words:

> That I have loved only you, surrendered my whole self reckless to you and nobody else. That I want you to love me back and show it to me. That I love the way you hold me, how close you let me be to you. I like your fingers on and on, lifting, turning. I have watched your face for a long time now, and missed your eyes when you went away from me. Talking to you and hearing you answer— that's the kick.
>
> But I can't say that aloud; I can't tell anyone that I have been waiting for this all my life and that being chosen to wait is the reason I can. If I were able I'd say it. Say make me, remake me. You are free to do it and I am free to let you because look, look. Look where your hands are. Now.

When I found him, I decided, I would sacrifice anything and everything for the man I loved.

I READ BELL HOOKS'S *ALL ABOUT LOVE* JUST AS OBTUSELY AS I did *Romeo and Juliet* and *Jazz*. *All about love* appealed to me because I thought it was the instructional guide to love that I had been so desperately looking for. And it was. Or, it could have been, if only I had taken hooks's real and actually very clear advice to heart instead of getting as far as halfway through her thoughts and then twisting them up with what I had decided Shakespeare and Morrison had already taught me.

At the beginning of her book, hooks quoted M. Scott Peck: "We do not have to love. We choose to love." She goes on to explain that healthy love is a verb, not a noun, and that how we treat our beloved, and what kind of treatment we accept back from them, is the real stuff that love is made of. Excellent, thoughtful, wise words.

Which I cast aside and refused to take into consideration.

Instead, I fixated on the word *choose* and the way it seemed to magically fit with a scene in *Jazz* that I couldn't stop thinking about, a scene between Joe and Dorcas where Joe declares that while he had fallen for Violet (quite literally, right out of a tree), he has now chosen Dorcas: "Nobody gave you to me. Nobody said that's the one for you. I picked you out. Wrong time, yep, and doing wrong by my wife. The picking out, the choosing. Don't ever think I fell for you, or fell over you. I didn't fall in love, I rose in it. I saw you and made up my mind."

My father fell for my mother. He made the grand gesture. Filled with passion and plans for their future, he flew across the world to declare himself and bring her home with him.

My mother chose my father. She watched him get down on one knee and thought, *I barely know him, but he is handsome and educated and he wants to bring me to America. So, why not say yes?*

In hindsight, neither of these choices seemed wise. My father fell for a beautiful smile. My mother chose what seemed to her a sensible option. Neither knew the other at all, really. Yet somehow, instead of learning anything from their mistakes, I decided that I would braid these concepts together. I decided that I would choose to fall.

Like my mother, I would be deliberate. I was going to find the right man, a man who fit me exactly, and I would be proactive about getting him. I would work toward our love the same way I worked at a job or my grades.

And then, like my father, I would fall. I would live and die for that man I had chosen. And, of course, he would also choose and fall for me.

I blithely decided that was what bell hooks would want me to do. Just like I ignored the fact that Romeo and Juliet were all of fourteen and ended up dead in what was essentially a giant misunderstanding; just like I skipped right over Joe choosing Dorcas and then promptly killing her, causing Violet to become violent and delusional; I ignored the fact that hooks wasn't telling me to wield a checklist and pick some stranger out of the crowd and make him my love. She was simply trying to get at the idea that love and abuse couldn't coexist. That love needed to be shown through your actions, and that your actions should be pure.

But I didn't care about these things—though I should have. (I wish I had. I am still learning this lesson.) What I wanted was to control love. I wanted to manifest it. I wanted it to be prescriptive. I would find the right man and choose him, and then we could be Romeo and Juliet, living (or dying) for only each other.

I didn't know what I wanted to be when I grew up. I

didn't know what I wanted to major in. I was barely keeping my head from flying off my own neck. But I knew what kind of man I wanted. And I knew what kind of relationship I wanted to have. I thought I had finally figured out what love should be.

And that's when I met, and chose, Chris.

CHRIS AND HIS FRIENDS CAME INTO THE DINER WHILE I was working the midnight shift. I immediately liked everything about him. He was tall and good-looking with a roller coaster of a smile. He wore glasses. He had a little bit of a New York City accent. He was confident and charming, twenty-four to my nineteen. He was preparing to go to law school.

He asked for my number, so I gave it to him, and within a couple of months I moved in with him (again, without my mom's knowledge or permission). I was confident that I'd made the right choice. He seemed to be everything I wanted. I imagined our life together. He had attended Howard, so I would transfer to Howard, too. He was going to be a lawyer, so I immediately started studying for the LSAT. We would be a power couple, he would take care of me, and I would be his trophy wife and helpmate.

I was sure that I was in love.

I very consciously chose, and then fell for, Chris. But what happens when you choose someone but they don't choose you back?

———

I HAD BEEN A LITTLE MOTHER PRACTICALLY MY ENTIRE life. Taking care of my brothers, stepping in for my own mom all those times she was working or too exhausted to rise from her bed. I had changed diapers and brushed teeth and cooked meals and did the dishes. I had read, and sung, and rocked. I had applied Band-Aids and kissed foreheads and soothed bad dreams. I had acted as a mother long before I could physically carry a child, while I was still trying to figure out what being a woman meant.

Chris never knew me as a mother, but he made me want to be a grown woman. And not just any woman—I wanted to be the woman he wanted. The woman he would choose. For about a year, I played house. I showed love the way I had been taught: I cared for him, I cooked for him, and I cleaned for him. I did whatever I could to make his life easier. I continued to hide him from my mother. I took whatever crumbs he gave me and tried to make a whole cake. I spent so much time trying to impress him. I wanted so badly to prove my worth. I studied his standard of feminine beauty. I straightened my hair. When he told me I needed to do something about my nails, I went to the salon and got acrylics. I was playacting adulthood. Trying on a life like it was a costume.

When Chris turned twenty-five, I decided to throw him a surprise party. A very adult and sophisticated surprise party. I was too young to legally drink, but I got one of his friends to buy alcohol and imagined myself confidently mixing cocktails to order. I put out chips and salsa, a vegetable tray and dip, deviled eggs, and olives. I invited all his friends and guided him into the room with my hand over his eyes. Everyone yelled "Surprise!" and then I smiled and looked up at him in what I imagined to be an adoring way, waiting for his kiss of thanks. He barely met my glance. Instead he beamed out his pleasure at his assembled friends (all much older than I was) as if *they* had planned and executed the party. Laughing, he stepped away from me and left me to mix drinks and refill trays and try not to seem too eager whenever someone bothered to talk to me, stretching my chubby baby cheeks into what I hoped was a mysterious and worldly smile.

CHRIS COULD BE KIND. BUT NOT KIND ENOUGH. CHRIS could be charming, but only when he wanted something from me. Chris did not take my youth or inexperience into consideration. He did not treat me well or help me grow. He accepted all I had to give him and never considered what I might want or need in return. I remember laying in bed with him and wailing in my head, *I choose you! Now you choose me!*

Even his friends, many of whom eventually became my friends, noticed the way he treated me. They used to take me aside like I was their little sister and ask me why I was settling for so little. They told me that I didn't need him, that I should go back to school, stand on my own two feet, that I was worthy of so much more.

But I just shook my head and told them they were crazy. Juliet didn't leave Romeo. Violet never gave up on Joe.

A FEW MONTHS AFTER I MOVED IN WITH CHRIS, I QUIT MY job as a hostess and started working as reading tutor for a local grade school. At the end of that year, they invited me to a sleepaway camp with the students. I was only there a couple of days when I got a tick bite and became violently ill.

Someone drove me back to D.C.—I was so feverish and miserable I couldn't even tell you who it was—and took me straight to a local ER. I told the person who had dropped me off that they could go, I would be fine. I had people who would take care of me.

I called Chris from my hospital bed. "I need you. I'm so sick. They don't know what's wrong with me. Can you please come?"

I must have been asleep when he arrived, because the next thing I remember was opening my eyes and finding him standing over me. I still felt so ill, but seeing his face gave me such relief. I had barely admitted it to myself, but there had been a moment when I'd wondered if he would actually show up.

I smiled at him and reached up to pat down my hair, painfully aware that I probably looked like shit. "Hey," I croaked.

"Hey." He shifted uncomfortably. "We have to talk."

AFTER CHRIS LEFT ME AT THE HOSPITAL, I WAS FAIRLY CER-tain that I would die. If not from the tick bite, then from my cracked and crumbled heart. I had never felt so vulnerable, so disappointed, so fucking stupid. I'd never understood how quickly things could turn.

Once I was discharged from the hospital, I found my way back to life. Still unable to admit to my mother what had happened, I moved in with a friend. During that summer, I decided I definitely didn't want to be a lawyer, but I did still want to go to Howard. It had been Chris's school, but before Chris, it was my father's alma mater, and that still meant something to me.

FOR AS LONG AS I COULD REMEMBER, I HAD STRAIGHTENED my hair. Hair in the Black community is a Thing, of course, with deep roots in colorism and respectability politics. And hair in the Nigerian community might even be more of a Thing, where any woman who dares wear her hair natural tends to be looked down on as slovenly or unkempt. So for most of my life I worked very hard at keeping my hair "presentable."

My mother approved of my straight hair. She believed in the power of beauty, and she thought straight hair was beautiful. She was beautiful herself—I was convinced that she could be Miss America if she wanted to—and that beauty had opened many doors for her over the years. But it didn't escape my notice that, while she had walked through most of those doors, she didn't necessarily like the rooms she found herself trapped inside of.

After I was accepted to Howard, I refused to care about what someone like Chris wanted me to be. I wanted to be strong. I wanted to be smart. I wanted to be kind. I wanted to be creative.

So that fall, after I moved into my dorm room, I tore the acrylics off my nails. I sat there for a long time, staring at myself in the mirror. It was the first time I could remember seeing the natural texture of my hair without the chemicals. I went to a local barber shop and after he was finished cutting my hair, my head felt light and cool. My eyes looked so big. My neck looked too long. For a moment, I worried that maybe I had gone too far and appeared almost masculine.

As I left the salon, I shivered and pulled up my collar, unused to the bite of cold air at the base of my neck, the way the wind nipped at my ears. I couldn't stop touching my head, marveling at how different and exposed I felt.

When I got back to my dorm, I immediately exchanged the small pearls in my ears for big hoops, put on a dark red lipstick, and did my lashes. And then I was happier with what I saw in the mirror. I'd wanted to give up my vanity, but first I needed to grow into this new presentation of who I was.

I needed to learn to love myself.

YOU CANNOT BE A YOUNG WOMAN AT HOWARD AND NOT be aware of the fact that this was the place where Chloe Anthony Wofford evolved into Toni Morrison. She attended the university from 1951 to 1955, and then she returned as a professor in 1958. It was at Howard where she wrote *The Bluest Eye*, the book that started her iconic writing career.

I like to look at pictures of Morrison as a young student. In the scholarly articles about her, it is always mentioned that she was a voracious reader and a brilliant academic, but not many people bother to note that she was absolutely stunning. She didn't spend her whole time at Howard with her nose in a book. She did theater; she was on the homecoming court. She took advantage of every opportunity, both academic and social, that Howard offered. I love one picture of her standing in front of the Blackburn University Center. She's probably not even twenty, wearing a fur coat, a purse dangling from one arm and a huge, beautiful smile on her face. She looks timeless. She looks at ease. She already looks like a shining star.

I think I know how she was feeling. If you are Black, and you come from a space where people don't see you, or where you were the only Black person in the room, or you have been tokenized, or simply forced to exist under the weight of low expectations, arriving at Howard can feel like deliverance. When you are suddenly surrounded by so many talented, dazzling Black people, and this multitude of brilliance instantly boosts your confidence and your own self-worth, that sensation of being alone, of being the only one, simply dissipates. Being Black and smart, Black and creative, Black and outspoken is the norm, not the exception, at Howard. And that general excellence works almost like osmosis. Most places in America are not designed for Black people to thrive—or even survive—in. The liberation of being in a place where you are expected to soar allows you to truly believe you are capable of doing absolutely anything.

Because why not? Look whose footsteps you are following in. Toni Morrison was here before you. I would continue to read more books by Morrison, including *Sula*, a story that meditated on what it meant to be free, Black, and a woman.

Sula's epigraph opens with my name and I took it as a sign: "Nobody knew my rose of the world but me. . . . I had too much glory. They don't want glory like that in nobody's heart." I had a habit for searching for meaning everywhere. I pretended Morrison had my heart in mind. Like *The Bluest Eye*, the novel is a story of two Black girls coming of age. Sula Peace and Nel Wright are more than friends, they are sisters. They share childhood dreams, dark secrets, and ultimately, precarious paths toward adulthood. From 1919 to 1965, we witness a lifetime of their beloved friendship. I wanted to be like Sula Peace. She helped me envision a life that could be luxurious, haughty, and filled with something other than self-sacrifice. Throughout the novel Sula is fearless, brave, intelligent; she is nobody's fool. The book seemed to center on sisterhood, survival, and how we all come to depend on one another in the end. Mother and daughter. Husband and wife. Best friends. Each relationship significant and full of demands; seeking love, loyalty, or simply escape. Nel's final cry of "'O Lord, Sula . . . girl, girl, girlgirlgirl" echoed in my mind.

All of Morrison's books are a lesson in transgressive art; she was uncompromising with her writing and captured the essence of Black life. In her early novels—*The Bluest Eye*, *Sula*, and *Song of Solomon*—she is exploring themes of Black girlhood, collective liberation, spiritual revival, and standards of beauty. Her stories are rich with folklore and the narratives are centered on Black identity. No matter the novel, the reader is confronted with moral complexity, mythology, and profound love. Pecola Breedlove. Sula and Nel. Baby Suggs.

Each character holding the rhythm and vivid history of Black people. Her fifth novel, *Beloved*, is dedicated to the "*Sixty Million and more*" people who died enslaved. Morrison's work transcended fiction, it is an embodiment of the Black experience—with all of its varied complexities and distinctions. Her books are layered with versatility and vulnerability, with references to slavery and the spiritually sublime. All of it filled me. *Girlgirlgirl.*

AS WE SLOWLY MARCHED UP GEORGIA AVENUE, I PULLED A hat over my hair, still a little self-conscious about my exposed neck, the fact that I had nothing to hide my face behind. It was early spring but still cold, and I carried a sign that I'd made with my roommate: BY ANY MEANS NECESSARY! We were surrounded by thousands of other Howard students: the Student Association, the African Student Union, the student government, the fraternities and sororities, the hierarchy of political action on campus. All these incredible microcosms of community that had come together to defend affirmative action, to protest this one thing that had an impact on us all.

All through my first year at Howard, I had been reading and thinking and slowly realizing that love—the foundational kind of love—was both smaller and bigger than the romantic sort of love I'd been raised to desire and expect.

There was the vital intimacy of self-love. Pleasing myself, admiring myself, allowing myself grace and understanding. Believing in my own worth.

And then there was this kind of love. The kind of spiritual love that happens when you are lifted up into a crowd, acting for the greater interest and a bigger cause.

We were a great body of young Black students, slowly moving past houses and businesses, holding up our signs, chanting, "Defend affirmative action!" People stopped and watched us, scratching their heads, wondering what we were protesting. It was so serious, but at the same time, so joyful.

And I remember feeling that, no matter how slow we might be moving, we were steadfast in our intentions and goals. We were inching forward with intent and dedication. I felt part of something bigger than me. I was part of a collective movement for the first time ever, and I realized that what we were doing could really make a difference. We might not see the results immediately, but there were newspaper reporters there, and newscasters, and people were watching, and we were capturing the community's attention.

It was a call to action. We were one body, one voice, even with all these individual identities. I had only ever felt this kind of sacred sense of unity in church, but church had never been this big, this loud, had never moved on its slow, deliberate feet in quite the same way.

I think people tend to mistake protesting for a heroic act. Of course, if a protest is met with violence, that violence can be heroically faced. But often, like on that day in D.C. — like most of the Black Lives Matter protests of these past few years — protest is just everyday people coming together, sharing a story and having a collective purpose. It is a reminder that we can't do things in isolation. That people have to depend on other people, not only for their input and intelligence and their ideas and strategy, but because you actually need those people to fill the streets. Just being a body can play a role. I could stand with my sign in the middle of Georgia Avenue, on my own, and that is one way to protest. But on that day in college, I stood with thousands of other people, and I felt the sun on the back of my neck, and I tipped my shorn head up to the sky, and I raised my voice with theirs. And I felt beautiful, oh, so beautiful, as I was lifted by the power, and the connection, and the energy that rocketed between us all. And I learned that a love story is different when it's told in a chorus.

DURING THAT FIRST YEAR AT HOWARD, I RE-READ *JAZZ* AND *all about love*. And with a little more wisdom, a little more maturity, and a little bit of heartbreak under my belt, I finally broke my habit of twisting words in order to make them fit what I wanted them to say. I learned to read carefully, critically, to take the time necessary to work through the harder ideas and phrases, to open up my mind and let the authors' words fizz through me and settle into my bones.

It was in this state of mind that I first read *The Black Woman: An Anthology* by Toni Cade Bambara. And somehow she crystallized everything Morrison and hooks had been trying to tell me for years.

Toni Cade Bambara wrote a little about love, yes, but

more importantly, she wrote about the depth of possibility and healing. She wrote about the need for equality between Black men and women. She made me look even further into the stereotypical masculine and feminine roles I had so wholeheartedly embraced. She made me face up to the fact that I was trying to emulate and re-create my own parents' marriage, positive that I could rewrite their bitter history if I just dropped all self-regard. I thought about the way I had willingly put myself into the role of supporter and helpmate with Chris. The way I had used love as an excuse not to do the hard work of figuring out what I really wanted. I was ashamed of the way I had decided to let a man take over my life. I realized that I didn't need to know who I was yet, nor did I need someone to tell me what to do. And that was okay. I would find my way at my own pace.

Grasping the true meaning of *Jazz* and *all about love* and reading Toni Cade Bambara raised me up and empowered me. Those books gave me a solid footing again. They forced me to think about my own manifestation and consciousness.

They made love clear.

I still had questions about love, of course. Maybe more than before, even. I still wanted security (that might be something I will never get over craving), but I was able to give up my dream of marrying rich. I was able to embrace the contradictions of who I was becoming. I realized that I could make the life I wanted without relying on a man, or my family, or even God. I just wanted to figure it out on my own.

If and when I looked for love again, I told myself that

I would still be vigilant in choosing what kind of love I wanted, and I would be brave enough to let myself fall, but I would also be wise enough to remember that I didn't need more than what I already inherently had.

I told myself to stop searching for Romeos or Joes.

And I knew that I would no longer be a Juliet or a Violet or a Dorcas.

I promised myself I would be William Shakespeare. I would be bell hooks. I would be Toni Morrison. I would be Toni Cade Bambara.

I would write my own story.

Because my life was already filled with love. There were messages of love in every book I opened and read. Words of love in every song I listened to. I saw love reflected in my community, in the faces and thoughts of my classmates and professors. I felt it from my friends. I felt it when we gathered as a political movement. I saw it beaming back at me from the mirror every morning.

Love has continued to arrive again and again in my lifetime, in all sorts of forms. And every time it appears, I treat it with more care. I know I will read Morrison and hooks and Bambara again and find even more truth about love in their words. I know I will continue to turn to their wisdom to teach me how to welcome love with proper reverence and awe.

And with their help, I will continue to choose love. I will close my eyes, and hold my arms out, and let myself fall.

CHAPTER SIX

Nikki Giovanni, *Like a Ripple on a Pond*

When I was seventeen years old, I recommitted myself to God. I had already been baptized twice as a child, but as a rigidly devout teenager, I thought it important that I cleanse myself again as an extra precaution. Our church was like a second home to me. Every Sunday morning, I attended services with my mother and brothers. My mother was even more devout than I was and determined to see that all of her children were safely saved. We joined in all the good work that was such a huge part of our church's identity, bringing food to the homeless and clothes to those who needed them, raising money with bake sales and car washes and raffle after raffle after raffle. Looking back now, I marvel at the fact that my family was surely just as poor as most of the people we were helping. But my mother fiercely believed in doing unto your neighbor, and my brothers and I would never question that tenet.

I played the bells for our church—the one musical instrument I ever mastered—standing in a line with the other girls, wearing little white gloves, as I waited patiently for my moment to snatch up my instrument and boldly ring one of the two notes I was capable of contributing to our hymn.

Though I never would have admitted to it, I definitely committed the sin of pride after my third baptism. Two of my girlfriends from school wrote me flowery notes, thanking me for recommitting myself to God, and this only added to my overbearing piousness. I walked around imagining myself as only a bell note or two away from being an outright saint. I took it all so seriously that when prom rolled around—a scandalous event where I imagined everyone was going to lose their virginity and have sex all over the place—I told my long-suffering, not-nearly-as-religious-as-me boyfriend that I couldn't go with him because the temptation would be too great. Instead, unwilling to give up my chance to put on a fancy dress and dance until my feet hurt, I asked T, a godly teen member of our church, to accompany me as a friend. (And the fact that T also looked like a younger, taller version of Blair Underwood had nothing to do with anything, I swear.) Blair—I mean, T—and I chastely danced the night away, and afterward, as all my friends ran off to drink at afterparties, I loudly announced that I was going home because I wanted to obey God's word and be a good person, and that's what a good person would do.

I STARTED COLLEGE FILLED WITH THE INTENTION OF CONtinuing on this righteous path, but, thrust into a group of people barely past pubescence, many of whom were away from their parents for the first time ever, I quickly realized that everything fun at college would have looked like sin back home.

For the first few weeks, at least, I behaved. I sat in my dorm room, earnestly praying for the souls of all my friends out there on campus who were, in my humble opinion, having way too much of a good time. They were drinking and sleeping around and getting high and testing all the boundaries of their newfound liberty, while I thinned my lips and shook my head and did my best to "live a life that spoke louder than words." But, unlike high school, nobody was sending me thank-you notes for my martyrdom. In fact, nobody was noticing me at all.

It wasn't long before I started to get bored and restless. And lonely.

I had been taught that faith is the belief in things unseen, but after watching another one of my friends happily get ready for a date I knew she wouldn't return from until the next morning (and secretly judging her the whole time), I couldn't help feeling that maybe I was talking to God, but He was definitely not bothering to say anything back.

I suppose it's easy to be religious when things are going well. You can say, "Oh, here's my abundance, here's my joy, here are the gifts that I have earned through my reverence." But when things go wrong and you're struggling? "Where is He? How is He caring for me right now? Why can't I see the reflection of His existence?"

I had worked so hard to be good. I literally imagined myself as checking off purity boxes: I had cast aside my boyfriend and gone to the prom with a godly boy. I had stayed away from sex and alcohol. I'd said my prayers and done good work and sat in my dorm room for days on end, waiting for the rewards that never arrived. "Right way, check! Right way, check! Right way, check!"

So what's up, God? Where were my rewards?

It didn't occur to me that looking at my relationship with my God as purely transactional was probably not the most faithful or healthy version of belief.

BY THE TIME I TRANSFERRED TO HOWARD UNIVERSITY OVER a year later, I'd cast aside any pretense of being a woman of God. I stopped regularly attending any kind of services. I hadn't even prayed in months.

And beyond all the trappings of worship I'd left behind, I'd also started thinking hard about the things in my religion that simply didn't add up anymore. I thought about my relatives in Nigeria. I'd always been taught that I should be worrying about their salvation. I had been told that the only way to avoid hell was to know a certain kind of gospel, to pray a certain way, to accept only Jesus into your heart. But the more I thought about it, the less sense it made. What if my relatives had never even had the chance to see a Bible? What if they practiced a traditional religion, like the religion that my own father had believed in, the religion of our ancestors? My father believed in both Christ and Abasi. Did that mean he was going to hell?

Not to mention the fact that my mother, the most truly

pious and godly woman I knew, couldn't seem to catch a break. She'd done nothing but follow the biblical rules as closely as possible, and in return she'd been saddled with two unhappy marriages, a lifelong struggle with her finances, and now, according to my brother Maurice, who regularly called me from home, there was something even more worrisome at play.

"She hasn't been out of bed in days, Glo," he whispered on the phone.

"Mom has always slept a lot," I said. "I'm sure she's just tired. She's doing too many double shifts."

He paused for a moment. "Maybe," he finally said.

"She'll be fine," I assured him. "She just needs a day off."

"Yeah." He sounded doubtful.

I hung up the phone determined not to think about it anymore, needing to believe that I was right—that my mom would be fine, just like she always was. I shook off the sound of my brother's worry so I could get back to what I considered my much bigger problems, trying not to listen to the little voice in my head that squeaked, *See? What's the point? All that praying, all that piousness, and your mother still can't get out of bed.*

HEARTSICK, WORRIED, AND DISILLUSIONED WITH THE FAITH I had been raised in, I started looking for enlightenment everywhere else. My journals at the time were filled with philosophical lists of things I did or did not believe in and inspirational quotations that I thought might lead me back into the light. I tried to read *In Search of Lost Time,* I did the heavy lifting with *Ulysses.* I scrawled notes on T. S. Eliot and John Keats and E. E. Cummings. But instead of lifting me up, these texts just made me feel even smaller and more in-significant.

Mixed into my rendezvous with all these white male ti-tans of literature were my sporadic attempts to come back to prayer. But these prayers sounded more like spurts of ques-tions: *Dear God, is this right? Like, is this the way people are actu-ally supposed to do stuff? Is this what adulthood is like? Is this what being in college is like? Is this what religion is like?*

But I never heard an answer. And it made me bitter.

I just wanted someone to tell me what to do.

I KNOW NOW THAT NOBODY HAS IT ALL FIGURED OUT. BUT at the time, I didn't take the fact that some people simply have more privilege and access than others—more resources, more luxury, more therapy—into consideration of my per-sonal existential crisis.

Occasionally a glimmer of a thought that sounded some-thing like, *You don't have time to be enlightened* would come to me. I was working two jobs and trying to keep my GPA up, and I was very busy hiding my unhappiness. When you're working that hard, your mind doesn't have much of a chance to sit with change. So even when I did force the time to read Emerson or Whitman or Thoreau, I could see the philoso-phy behind their words, but more relevantly, I saw so much of their idleness, too.

I didn't have the leisure to take long daily walks in nature or to spend my afternoons lingering over lunch and discussing the finer points of Eastern philosophy with like-minded friends. (Nor did I have wives or servants to relieve me of having to spend any of my brainpower thinking about menial tasks.) I was limited to reading about these things in fits and snatches, or hoping that I would get it through absorption or osmosis. Or simply making it up as I went along.

WHEN I FOUND NIKKI GIOVANNI, I DIDN'T KNOW THAT I had found my path back to God. I responded to Giovanni's work right away—when I read her poems, it sounded like someone talking to me. There was no air of pretention, and unlike some of the other, more canonical writers I had been trying to squeeze answers out of, Giovanni's language never read as overly academic. Her voice was light. It had a very carefree touch to it. It felt like a friend talking to you. Reading her work, I felt like she was telling me her story one-on-one. And when I first listened to her album *Like a Ripple on a Pond*, an experimental combination of her spoken word poetry and traditional gospel music sung by the New York Community Choir, I didn't suddenly feel wise so much as young again. The doors of my consciousness weren't blown wide open, but I felt a small, joyful sense of liberation from the slog I was experiencing in my day-to-day life.

I didn't have much exposure to gospel music or the powerful, resounding church choirs it emanated from. Playing the bells was not quite the same as swaying and shouting and singing for the glory of God. I thought of gospel music as *"The Color Purple* music." I loved the tingle I felt as I listened to it, and at first I just listened to Giovanni's album as a pick-me-up. It gave me a shot of energy in the morning as I was getting ready to get out the door.

WHEN I TRANSFERRED TO HOWARD, I STARTED TO ATTEND services at Howard's Andrew Rankin Memorial Chapel. The services were nondenominational and by no means compulsory, but they were a historic part of the institution that I was determined not to miss. There was a revolving cast of speakers and preachers leading the church, and you never knew who you might encounter or what they might choose to pontificate upon.

One Sunday morning, there was a pastor (and I wish I could remember his name) who was lecturing on James Baldwin. He was at the pulpit, giving accolades to Baldwin's work, talking about how his words were so revolutionary, instructing us in the reverence that was due. And I loved the lecture. I'd just finished reading *Go Tell It on the Mountain* and was studying Baldwin in earnest, and I had already recognized him as a writer who would shake my world. But after chapel, all I could think on the walk back home was, *Who else?* Was there any other literary figure this preacher could have talked about on the pulpit?

Back in my dorm, my eyes fell on a copy of *Gemini* sitting on my bed. I had been reading it with the greatest of pleasure, and it came to me: "Oh my God, of course. Nikki Giovanni."

Even though I had grown up with Reverend Roxanne at the head of my chapel back in Arlington, I still thought of church as a male-dominated space. Most preachers were male. The scripture spent most of its time on men. It was Paul and Moses and Matthew, never Mary Magdalene. So much of what was directed to the women of the congregation was built around the idea of submission, and that had never felt like a comfortable space for me. But perhaps seeing the Reverend Roxanne at the pulpit had prepared me to respond to Giovanni standing at the forefront of the choir. Giovanni's presence and her words, her powerful voice, answered my longing to see women as faith leaders, to see women uplifted in worship instead of told to submit.

I STARTED TO LISTEN TO *LIKE A RIPPLE ON A POND* ON REPEAT. I played it in the morning when I was trying to find the energy to start my day. I played it at night as I drifted off to sleep, letting the sound of the music, the rhythm of it, seep into my subconscious as I dreamed.

It soothed me in a way that I hadn't known I needed to be soothed. It felt like the singers in the chorus cared for me. And Giovanni's voice was even more of a balm. Her lyrics were familiar to me in all the biblical ways, about overcoming and feeling love and feeling the power of God's perseverance and His resilience, but they had the added elements of Giovanni's poetic voice, her powerful, unapologetic womanhood, her insistence on not limiting faith and enlightenment to a male-dominated world.

Giovanni's lessons entered my soul like a soft, much-needed rain. I thought I was listening to the album because the music made me happy, gave me the tingles, but what it really gave me was permission to envision a spiritual life that was my own, and not one I just imitated because my parents instructed me to. The power of Giovanni's creativity allowed me to see that there could be other ways of praising God and acknowledging my sense of self. Spirituality could ignite my curiosity without being so conservative.

I had always thought of religion as a series of rules to be followed, a dictated and inflexible list of behavior that needed to be checked off before you were given your ultimate reward. But Nikki Giovanni was a master of playing with form and using her intelligence to help us understand that we can be okay with our neuroses. I didn't know that religion could give what Giovanni was teaching me—that it was okay to be weird and awkward and uncomfortable. It was okay not to know something. It was okay to ask a lot of questions. In my previous religious settings, and in my general upbringing, those things were not encouraged. Morality was either black or white, right or wrong, normal or not normal. But Giovanni didn't hew to *either/or*. She was all about *and*. Listening to her experiment with poetry and music on this album, taking two different things and putting them together, showed me that my spiritual life could consist of the same flexibility. The God I found through Giovanni didn't care if I did or didn't lose my virginity at prom. That God didn't need me to worry about the state of my father's eternal soul because he still kept to some of the old ways. That God knew that we humans were stumbling through the dark, making mistakes, just trying to figure it out, and He loved us even more for it.

MANY YEARS LATER, WHEN MY WORK AT WELL-READ BLACK Girl allowed me access to many of my literary heroes, I was privileged to have several conversations with Nikki Giovanni. The thing that always lingered for me after I spoke with her was the sense of her absolute openness and curiosity. She never seemed to be trying to impress or project her ideas onto me. She truly seemed more interested in guiding me to explore my own ideology.

Back when I was a reading specialist, I had often used Giovanni's poetry with my students. I felt she was an incredible model when it came to intergenerational relationships. She always invited younger folks into the conversation, and she seemed to find real joy in helping them make connections and see patterns. And years later, when I interviewed her at the Well-Read Black Girl Festival, I realized that so much of that came from a place of fierce, pure inquiry. She simply took joy in discovering other people's minds.

When Giovanni was younger, especially during the civil rights movement and after Dr. King was assassinated, she was considered more militant, more radical, and more aggressive in nature than her persona as an elder seems today. When I asked her if she regretted any of the combativeness of her past, she laughed and shook her head. "Maybe now I wouldn't say the same things I said when I was twenty," she said. "Maybe I now see things in a less stringent way, but I am proud of the work I made and the friction that it caused and the ideas that disrupted systems. They were my foundation."

Hearing her say that made me think about my own spiritual growth. Like Giovanni's political militancy, the church I had been brought up in had been unbending in its rules and philosophy, and so I had been equally intractable in my beliefs. But as Giovanni had grown older, she had found ways to include not bigger things, exactly, but more things into her worldview. Her mind had become broader and more accepting. She had learned to look beyond the narrowness of what she thought she already knew and take in the miracle of variation. And her wise, expansive outlook gave me a model to expand my own constricted spiritual beliefs.

Giovanni taught me that spirituality and prayer could be so much more than something I did on my knees within the four walls of a church. She taught me that prayer could be poetry and song and celebration. It was a way to show my gratitude to God, but also to myself. It was a way to acknowledge the big and the small, the known and unknown. It was a way to consecrate waking up every morning. It was a way to revel in God's goodness. It was a way to give thanks. To ask for protection. To practice supplication. Listening to Giovanni's album was a prayer. Reading her poetry was a prayer.

Those conversations I was so lucky to have with her? They were a kind of prayer as well.

So I thank God for Nikki Giovanni's words. I thank God for her voice and her wisdom and that big, beautiful brain that she so generously shares with us. I thank God for the pure fearlessness of her work. I thank God that Giovanni had the audacity to be brazen, to be unafraid, to be proud, to light the way for those of us who needed not just a candle but a torch. I thank God for Nikki Giovanni, and I thank Nikki Giovanni for my God.

CHAPTER SEVEN

Alice Walker, *The Color Purple*

I was nineteen years old and a sophomore in college, and my roommate Gimari and I were watching *The Color Purple*. We found the movie, already halfway played through, while aimlessly flipping channels one Sunday afternoon. It didn't matter that we had missed the beginning, we had both seen this film more times than we could count. I could practically recite it by heart, could close my eyes and unspool the plot in my mind, backward and forward. Gimari and I had an unspoken agreement; if it was on, we stopped and watched, and we could pick it up from whatever scene, the way old friends could pick up a conversation where they last left off, no matter how long they had been apart.

This day, we watched as Shug, played by Margaret Avery, shimmied in her red spangled dress and peacock feather headpiece while she crooned "Celie's Blues (Sister)" to an impossibly sweet and shy Whoopi Goldberg, who played Celie. I knew that, as I took this movie break for myself, my family was dealing with a lot. My mother was essentially entombed in what used to be my bedroom, unable to get out of what used to be my bed. She had lost maybe a third of her body weight, and she hadn't spoken for weeks, drifting in a place that I didn't understand and had begun to resent. There was hard trouble in our family. Something had gone very, very wrong with my mother, and I spent nearly every night panicking, trying to figure out *what to do*. But at that moment, I was watching *The Color Purple* with my friend and marveling at just how beautiful Whoopi Goldberg was, her radiant smile and fine bright eyes, her glowing brown skin and graceful hands. I felt nothing but peace as I watched Celie fall in love with Shug all over again on my television set.

TROUBLE DOESN'T ALWAYS COME ALL AT ONCE. SOMETIMES it seeps through in little unnoticeable drips, like a leak in the roof, pooling just under the surface until the ceiling suddenly gives in and comes crashing down upon your head.

That's the way it was with my mother.

Growing up, my brothers and I had become used to her physical absence. She worked long hours as a nurse, usually on the night shift, and even when she was home she was often sleeping or in a state of near exhaustion. But in the moments when she was present, she was *really* there. She had opinions about everything. She talked nearly nonstop. My mother was filled with overwrought, intense emotion, and that emotion was as much a part of our home as the walls around us and the floor under our feet.

Looking back, I can now understand that when my

mother lost her temper (which was often, and sudden, and usually over very small things), it was undoubtedly because she was so overtaxed to begin with. She had suffered through the loss of connection with her family and country of origin, the end of her marriage and then the sudden disappearance of my father, an emotionally abusive second marriage of convenience, financial stress, extremely limited resources, a chronic lack of sleep, raising three children on her own, not to mention the way immigrants and Black women were routinely treated in America. She had martyred herself to the cause of raising her little family, sacrificing her own well-being and self-care to our constant needs and demands, and she had no one—absolutely no one—she could turn to for relief. In retrospect, it was not surprising that an incident as small as Maurice forgetting to take out the garbage or me leaving a dish in the sink could send her into an uncontrollable rage. She had no bandwidth, no reserves, and even the most minuscule irritant must have felt like the end of her extremely frayed rope.

Still, as quick as she was to lose her temper, she was equally adept at finding a deep and celebratory joy. Before my mother's depression, she had an easy laugh, a bright and gorgeous smile, and a way of approaching even the most difficult disasters with a sense of optimism that sustained us all. She loved new beginnings. I have inherited this trait from her. Perhaps it evolved as a desperately needed coping mechanism, but no matter how badly something ended, my mother would always present it to us as the possibility of a clean slate, a brighter future, a chance to leave behind what was broken and move toward something whole. It was an extraordinary ability, a superpower, really. She truly believed that, despite the crumbs we were given, the deep disappointments and gigantic disasters that we faced, better things were always on the way.

I should have realized something was wrong when her big emotions, the joy and the anger, slowly became more and more muted. I should have known that the exhaustion my mother regularly felt—the kind of weariness that could be addressed with a weekend off, a bubble bath, a cup of hot tea—was very different than this sickness that arrived to cloud her brain and take away the light in her eyes. But I was young, and self-involved, and away from home for the first time, so I didn't see that our family was facing something unknown and terrifying, something that would change our lives in a very permanent way.

THE MOTHERS IN THE FILM OF *THE COLOR PURPLE* ARE ALL dead or missing or taken from their children. Celie and Nettie lose their mother shortly after Nettie is born. Celie's children are stolen from her, and she loses her chance to mother them. Sofia is incarcerated and torn away from her children. Shug's struggle is with her preacher father, and her mother is never mentioned. The adoptive mother of Celie's children, Corrine, dies while in Africa. It was hardly surprising that I was particularly drawn to this story in a time when it felt like my own mother had disappeared. Of course, her physical presence, her body in my bed, her refusal to eat, and most of all, her silence, filled my apartment and weighed on my mind. But the absence of her strong, inquisitive nature, her sharp sense of humor, her wide smile, and even her fitful and critical anger—all the things that made her the woman I knew as my mom—felt like a nearly unbearable loss. Watching *The Color Purple* sometimes seemed like the only way to numb that particular pain.

Just as Celie had Nettie, her sister and soulmate, I had Gimari. I had come into Howard as a transfer student in my sophomore year, a difficult transition because everyone else had already found their cliques and friends as first-year students. As social as I was, nothing daunted me more than the possibility that I might not have friends. But Gimari, who I met in my Media Production class, embraced me right away. She was smart and funny and beautiful; she was tall, with a dark complexion and almond eyes. When I first saw her, I thought she must be West African, specifically from Sierra Leone or Senegal. But when I asked her, she shook her head.

"Excuse me, but what are you talking about? Why do I have to be from Africa? I'm from Seattle!"

For a moment I worried I had somehow insulted her beyond repair. But then I explained that my family was from Nigeria, and we fell into a long, passionate conversation about what it meant to be African, and what it meant to be American, and what it was like to be first generation. From that moment on, Gimari became the sister I'd always wanted growing up.

She took me to parties, and we hung out in the yard on campus, and she introduced me to all her friends. Sometimes

I would sit in her dorm room, agonizing over some impossible-to-solve problem or decision I needed to make, and Gimari would haul out her Bible, crack it open, and stab her finger at whatever random sentence it happened to land on. It could have been pure fire and brimstone, it could have been a list of who begat whom, but Gimari would interpret it in such a way that it gave me every answer I needed, even as we giggled our way through her far-fetched translations.

Not long after we met, we moved out of our dorm rooms and took a tiny off-campus apartment in the basement of a beautiful townhouse owned by a West Indian man who lived upstairs from us. Neither I nor Gimari had much money—we barely had any furniture and were living off of dollar pizza and ramen—but we had a TV, and that's where we discovered our mutual love of *The Color Purple*.

Alice Walker was a hero to us both; the book had been a touchstone throughout our teenage years, and the film marked the first time we had ever seen an almost entirely Black cast in a big-budget Hollywood movie. We knew that there had been criticism of the production, that Spielberg had downplayed the relationship between Shug and Celie, that there were problems with the way Black men were portrayed, that some critics had felt that the movie was too sentimental and had gutted the intensity of Walker's original story. But those things didn't really matter to me or Gimari. Not compared to the fact that the breathtakingly gorgeous women cast in this movie weren't chosen for their European standard of beauty, or that Alice Walker had final cut and had insisted that at least half the crew be either women or people of color. That Oprah was in it! Oprah before anyone really knew who Oprah was! That the story tackled racism and rape and domestic abuse and poverty and yet still found its way to Black joy. We started regular viewings of the film. Each scene aligned with our growing friendship. Sometimes we'd shout "Celie! Nettie!" in unison, a warm and familiar greeting every Black girl knows by heart. We'd give each other a glance and whisper, "Harpo, who dis woman?" when someone looked at us sideways on campus. We'd sing, "All my life I had to fight" when feeling disappointment over a recent breakup or bad grade. We'd sit side by side on the futon, silently mouthing along as Shug and Celie strolled through that sun-filled field of wildflowers and Shug told Celie, "I think it pisses God off if you walk by the color purple in a field and don't notice it."

That little apartment was my own field of flowers. I felt like a true adult in that space. I felt like I had all the freedom in the world.

WHEN I WENT BACK HOME AT WINTER BREAK, I COULD vaguely sense that something was wrong. The air in that apartment felt heavy and still, but I couldn't puzzle out what the problem was, exactly. My brothers seemed the same, and I was overjoyed to see them. My mother's second marriage had finally ended almost a year back, and the absence of my stepfather in our lives should have felt like sweet relief. But something was off with my mother, something more than her usual depletion after a long working day. It was a feeling she brought into the room with her, like a cloud that wouldn't lift. And the things that normally would have lightened her aspect—a delicious meal, a funny joke, a good song—didn't seem to make any difference to her at all.

I thought it was financial. Growing up, she had done an extremely good job of hiding our poverty from me and my brothers, but as I grew older, I became more and more aware of the financial strain looming over our family. And I knew that certain bills had not been paid—Maurice had reported this to me. Financial insecurity was stressful and worrisome, of course, but not new, and there was some relief when I decided that the ripple of disaster I'd been feeling was really nothing more than our usual problem keeping the lights on.

When I left to go back to school, I was worried, but I still had no idea just how far below normal my mother had already plunged.

Then Maurice called. It seemed that Mom had lost her job months ago, and they were being evicted.

HOME HAS ALWAYS BEEN A TRICKY SUBJECT FOR ME. WE never owned our own house while I was growing up. We moved from two-bedroom apartment to two-bedroom apartment, taking what we could afford, and cramming us all in even as our family grew bigger and my mother's income became smaller. More than anything, I longed for the stability of a family home, a rambling house where we each had our own bedroom and didn't have to wait to use the bathroom and had a big yard to play in. I wanted space enough for everyone, with hidden corners and soft, sunny spots to curl up and read.

Even though we rented, my mother had a way of making things feel homey. She had a keen eye for interior design, and it was important to her that our house was stylish and pin-neat. And she always, *always* paid the rent on time. So it had never even occurred to me that she could be evicted. But still, I saw the problems we were facing as something we could solve in a fairly straightforward manner. My mother and Tunde moved to D.C. to stay with an old friend of my mother's, a woman who was close enough to us to call Auntie, while Maurice stayed behind with family friends to finish school. I was still worried, of course, but this seemed like the right path. My mother would save money while she searched for work. I knew she would get a new job, just as she always had before. Then, once she had a paycheck or two, we would find an apartment for her and Tunde. Things would surely continue on in a familiar manner.

In the meantime, Gimari and I fixed up our little home. It was hardly bigger than our combined dorm rooms had been, but the fun of painting a wall a color we both loved or hanging a new poster made us feel independent and worldly. I loved my new life as someone who got to make choices, even small, basic ones, based entirely on my own whims.

And we continued to watch as Celie moved into her new house after her marriage to Mister, tackling the disgustingly dirty kitchen he presented her with, turning the neglected home from dross to gold.

——

EVERYTHING BECAME MUCH MORE REAL WHEN MY PHONE rang one evening and Auntie was on the line.

"Come and get your mother," she said. "I am done. There's something wrong with her and she cannot live here anymore."

My mother's relationship with her best friend stretched back years. They had been there for each other through all sorts of hardship. It was unthinkable to me that Auntie would turn her back on my mom. But Auntie continued to rant, not giving me details but saying that my mother had behaved so badly that Auntie thought there was a good chance she was actually possessed by a demon.

As my mother got worse, this was something that would come up again and again among the expatriate crowd of Nigerians that we had always been able to count on. Mental health issues were not readily understood or accepted. If someone was acting oddly or obviously struggling, the answer was almost always to pray, to look toward God, to bring in a priest for an exorcism if necessary.

The longer I listened to Auntie, the clearer it became; the friendship between my mother and her was irretrievably broken, and our last lifeline had been removed. My mother and Tunde had no place to go.

I turned to Gimari, my sister and friend and sometimes savior, and asked if my mother and brother could come and stay with us for a while. Just until things got better?

She didn't bat an eye. She came from a huge, loving family and her own background of hardships, and she knew exactly what I was asking and why. "Of course. This is your home, and your family is always welcome here."

———

ONE OF THE STORY ARCS OF *THE COLOR PURPLE* LETS US FOL-
low Celie as she finds her voice. As an actress, Whoopi Goldberg did so much with silence. Her beautiful face was
expressive enough to carry the film even if she never uttered
a word, but I remember the first time the grown-up Celie
speaks in the film—the surprisingly low, sweet gravel of her
voice as she reads *Oliver Twist* out loud to herself while rocking in her chair. The way the film builds and builds Celie's
confidence, until she is finally allowed her glorious, scathing
speech at the dinner table, stabbing that knife into the wood
just in front of Mister's plate and cursing him and her terrible stepchildren, shaking off her fear, and finally telling them
just what she really thinks and feels.

Sometimes it seemed like my mother followed an opposite trajectory. When I picked her and Tunde up from
Auntie's, my normally loquacious mom—the woman who
had never held back an opinion, thought, or emotion—
stared straight ahead with dead, flat eyes and refused to answer my questions, only mumbling under her breath when
pressed, and sometimes even using a pad and pen to write
down her answers. This was chilling. I didn't believe in demons or possession, but I almost wished that I could. At
least it would give me an explanation for what I was seeing.
I had absolutely no context to understand what was happening to her.

When we got back to my apartment, she drifted about
like a ghost, grunting and shuffling. I was disgusted and

frustrated. Why was she allowed to disconnect from our difficult reality? How was it fair that she was suddenly demanding my constant care? The thing is, I thought she had control over what was happening to her. I thought that her behavior and symptoms were a choice. I thought she could just decide to get better, and that she'd get up one morning and be herself again.

But, of course, she wouldn't—or rather *couldn't*—make that choice, so I reached for whatever solutions I could think of. I took her to multiple doctors, hoping to find someone who could tell me what was wrong. Surely they would see this mumbling and confused woman and be able to diagnose and cure her. But some sort of instinctual self-preservation always seemed to kick in when my mother was faced with authority. She would walk into the exam room and immediately spring back into her old self. It was astounding to me, seeing the light turn on in her face, hearing the words pour out of her lips. "I am fine," she would say, rolling her eyes at my insistence that she needed help. "I am perfectly healthy!" And the doctors, seeing no evidence to the contrary, would inevitably agree, leaving me to walk out with a woman who switched back to shuffling zombie mode the minute we left the building.

Remember how Celie begins to evolve and shine brightly in *The Color Purple*? The way that her clothes and hair become more and more precise and colorful as the movie progresses? I thought that I could work the same magic on my mother. She had always been proud of her appearance, tending to herself the same way she tended to our house, but now she was slipshod and sloppy. Her hair had gone completely gray; she would wear the same outfit day after day if I didn't remind her to change. So I decided to give her a makeover. It brings tears to my eyes to remember how innocent and foolish I was, my simple hope that if I changed my mother's appearance, it would somehow change everything. I dyed her hair back to black. I took her to a used clothing store and found a tailored suit. I sat her down and plucked her neglected brows, applied color to her unnaturally pale cheeks, carefully traced lipstick over her dry lips. When I was finished, she sort of looked like the mother I had known— a woman who could get a job, find an apartment, care for her children—except for the fact that her precisely made-up eyes were still empty and flat and refused to meet mine, that her lipsticked mouth worked in a twitching, nervous way, that her hands twisted in her lap as if by their own volition.

After that day, she went completely mute. She took to bed and stayed there, her voice completely gone.

Days turned into weeks turned into months.

It would be years before I heard my mother's voice again.

THE PENULTIMATE SCENE IN *THE COLOR PURPLE* TAKES PLACE in a small white church where Shug's father, who had turned his back on his daughter and her sinful ways, presided as the preacher. Shug still adored him, though, and tried repeatedly to reconnect and make him admit that she was still the daughter that he loved so well. It is Sunday morning and Shug, who is performing at Harpo's juke joint, hears the church choir singing what she thinks of as *her* song, "God's Trying to Tell You Something." She leads a group of people from the club into the church, singing all the way, until her voice and the choir's voice are one, and her father embraces her with tears in his eyes.

I adored that scene. It captivated me in every way. The beautiful uproarious sound; that room crammed with dazzling Black people, everyone singing and dancing; the healing that happens between Shug and her lost father. Watching it just gave me this incredible feeling of being transported, of leaving behind what had become my overcrowded apartment and the dark, hopeless cloud my mother had brought with her into my home.

I think, for many Black women, watching that film was a revelation. We had never seen ourselves centered like that before. We had never seen ourselves presented with so much beauty and strength. We had never been given that kind of particular voice or platform to tell our stories. Watching it reminded me what Black womanhood—Black life—could be at its most empowered and joyful. The way we could conquer almost anything with our eternal hope for something better.

Watching it reminded me of my mother, intact and whole in my memory, once again showing me how to gather up the broken pieces of our difficult and complicated life, teaching me to rearrange those shards until we could view them in a new way. That scene, that song, that magnificent film made me remember that there was a way to reframe heartbreak and failure and pain until it transformed into a vision of a future that shined with light and promise and optimism.

So whenever *The Color Purple* was on, Gimari and I would drop what we were doing, turn away from the small, silent woman huddled and suffering in the back room, and allow ourselves to be taken into a world where even the worst was overcome. Where the future could be bright, where loved ones were reunited, where Celie was finally given a house and home of her own. Where even the meekest people learned how to raise their voices and be heard, where there were fields of purple flowers dazzling us in the streaming sunlight. Where pain and silence were just temporary moments in the greater arc of our joy.

CHAPTER EIGHT

James Baldwin, *The Fire Next Time*, "The Doom and Glory of Knowing Who You Are"

You think your pain and your heartbreak are unprecedented in the history of the world, but then you read.

—JAMES BALDWIN

I t was Rodney King who taught me that my little brother was not safe in America. I was nine years old when King's beating at the hands of the LAPD and the subsequent riots in Los Angeles were broadcast. I was still too young to be particularly interested in the nightly news, but I noticed the way my parents grew still and tense as they watched the television, and I instinctually understood that something both painful and important had happened. I remember catching a glimpse of Rodney King's battered face and turning away in shock, but not before the image of his bruises and cuts, his bright red, bloody eye and swollen mouth, fixed itself permanently upon my imagination.

This was before the twenty-four-hour news cycle that we have today, so the reports on King were relatively short, usually just one small segment anchoring the hour of evening news. But even after the news was over and the television turned off, I listened as my parents—and then my teachers at school—continued to discuss the situation in hushed, hard voices for days after.

My view of the world was very simple back then. There was good and bad, right and wrong, and very little in between. I thought the bad were punished and that the good would be protected. I believed in justice, and I thought it was available to everybody who deserved it. So it shook me to realize that Rodney King did not deserve what had happened to him. He was not a dangerous criminal or a bad man. Rodney King was beaten by the police simply because he was a Black man.

Up until then, I had never considered the police to be anything but a force for good. We had police officers embedded in our school, but they were friendly, smiling; sometimes they even offered us candy. They were also the ultimate authority, and my parents had done a very thorough job of making sure that I always respected and trusted authority. I thought that the police were there to keep me out of harm's way, that they were on our side. But after Rodney King, I began to realize that I had been seeing things wrong, that the police, who I had always thought were there to serve and protect, could actually be dangerous in their own right. That if something happened to me—or most especially, to my little brother Maurice—if we needed help, it was no longer safe to go to a police officer, because they could, and maybe even most likely *would*, beat you. Now when I saw the police at school—the same seemingly friendly men who smiled at me and waved just like they always had—my body tensed, and I felt a little shudder of fear trickle down my back.

I remember watching Maurice one day—he was around six or seven then, and he had recently developed a habit of standing at our front window and enthusiastically waving at anyone who came by on the street. He'd been doing it all day, waiting eagerly until someone drove or walked by, and then thrusting his little body halfway out over the ledge, his feet on tiptoe, barely staying on the floor, and smiling and waving and shouting "Hi! Hello! Hi!" until the stranger outside waved back and became his friend. I thought it was cute, the way he wanted to be seen and connect, but when I saw a police cruiser roll up at the red light on our corner and Maurice started to lean out the window just like he had already done dozens of times that day, I felt an enormous pulse of fear. I made a dive for my little brother, pulling him to the floor and out of sight, desperately whispering, "That's the police! That's the police! Get down! You're gonna get in trouble!"

And I wasn't even thinking about real crime. I was thinking that Maurice could be beaten for being too loud, or not crossing the street in the right place, or fooling around, or leaning out the window and waving with too much enthusiasm.

WHEN I WAS TWELVE, THERE WAS A BOY IN MY CLASS AT school named Martinez, and he had a younger brother in

Maurice's class named Willie. For some reason Willie and Martinez started picking on Maurice. At this point our father had disappeared, and sometimes I think that his absence created a deep hunger in Maurice to be liked and included, especially by other boys. He always gravitated toward teams and clubs, he worked hard to fit in, and he was incredibly charming and eager to please. But for whatever reason, his charm didn't seem to work on Willie and Martinez, and one day I stumbled upon little Willie whaling away on my brother in the schoolyard with Martinez on the sideline, egging him on.

It was my job to protect my younger brothers. I carried this responsibility deep in my bones; it was as integral to my identity as my eye color or my first name. Whether it was the police, or my stepfather, or that nasty little kid and his big brother, I did my absolute best to come between my little brothers and anything that could possibly harm them. So when I saw Willie beating up on Maurice, I yelled at him to leave my brother alone, and then, when Willie didn't stop, I rushed in, shoved him away, and bent over to help Maurice up.

Willie was a mean, tough little kid, though, and apparently he was not done with this fight, because as I straightened up, he charged at me and bit me right on the boob.

It makes me laugh now, thinking about it. That little kid—he was five or six years younger than me—acting like a tiny, rabid monster. But at the time, I was hurt and humiliated. I had only recently started to wear a training bra, and my injury made me feel like Willie had exposed me in some way, like people would now know where my weaknesses were. Like despite the fact that I was growing bigger and stronger, puberty—my shift into womanhood—had left me even more vulnerable than I had been before.

Still, Maurice needed my protection. So I ignored my own pain and came right back out swinging at little Willie. I wasn't going to let this kid or anyone else hurt my brother. I was there as Maurice's compass, his alibi, his conscience, and his protector. I was his big sister, and I truly thought that if I stayed vigilant, I could keep him from all harm.

WHEN I READ JAMES BALDWIN'S *THE FIRE NEXT TIME,* IT FELT like testimony. I first opened it more than thirty-five years after its publication in 1963, when I was twenty years old, but there was nothing in Baldwin's words, point of view, or philosophy that felt dated. It was urgent, true, and still completely applicable to the life my brothers and I were facing. In a letter to his nephew, Baldwin wrote,

> This innocent country set you down in a ghetto in which, in fact, it intended that you should perish. Let me spell out precisely what I meant by that, for the heart of the matter is here, and the root of my dispute with my country. You were born where you were born, and faced the future that you faced because you were black, and *for no other reason*.

My brothers' lives would, indeed, be shaped a certain way because they were Black and *for no other reason,* and my own life had already been formed by the expectation that Black women could and should move the earth to protect the Black men in their lives—because we were the only ones who cared enough to do so.

When I read Baldwin's words, I saw Rodney King's broken face, and I suddenly understood the anxiety that brutal incident had triggered in me. I began to understand the feelings that had welled up in me as a little girl when I realized that Maurice and Tunde could be hurt in that same way. Baldwin gave me the vocabulary to describe that helpless impulse to try to protect the people you love from a system that you can't control.

The beginning of Baldwin's book is that letter to his fifteen-year-old namesake nephew, meditating on the insidious history of racism in America and how it would shape "Big James's" life, taking the time to wonder about what his young nephew's fate might be. I felt enervated, thinking about how little had changed between the time of Baldwin's experiences and my own, but I also felt a sense of urgency and rebellion; I was hell-bent on proving that, with enough care, time, and vigilance, I could somehow shape and control my brothers' particular fate. If I tried hard enough, I could order the steps my brothers took and keep them on the right path, insulated and safe.

And if that meant I had to fight for them the same way I had to fight little Willie, I was going to do that. If I needed to pull my younger brothers from the window and teach them to talk a certain way or move a certain way so they wouldn't seem suspicious or out of place, I was going to

do that, too. I hounded Maurice to stop wearing oversized
T-shirts and sagging pants. I evoked the name of Rodney
King loudly and often, hoping that his story would somehow teach my brothers that they had to be as respectable as
possible so that they could walk safely through this world.

Maurice was gentle and curious, fun-loving and efferves-
cent. He liked basketball and soccer and wrestling. We used
to make up songs together and write funny letters to each
other. He was playful and silly and filled with joy, but I now
understood that very few people, outside of those who knew
him intimately and had watched him grow up, would recognize these things about him. I knew that, as he grew, America would willfully and ignorantly misunderstand who he
was, do its best to strip him of this joy—and perhaps things
even more essential than that.

IT WAS PAST MIDNIGHT WHEN THE PHONE RANG. I DIDN'T
recognize the number, and normally I would have ignored
the call, but it was late enough to spark both curiosity and
worry, so I answered.

It was Maurice, calling me from jail.

He didn't have time to give me many details. He just told
me that he was in jail, in Baltimore, and that he needed me
to bail him out.

"Can you come get me?" he said. His voice wobbled, and
I felt my heart crack open.

"Yes, of course, yes," I answered. Then, thinking of all the
procedural crime shows I had watched over the years, I

added, "Don't do anything. Don't talk to anyone. Just wait. I'll be there soon."

Maurice was a freshman at Morgan State in Baltimore. I was a junior at Howard. Tunde was a freshman at boarding school, a decision we made when it proved evident our mother couldn't take care of him. She had been living with me, locked into her own silent world, for over two years now. My father had been gone for more than a decade.

I had no adults to turn to, no one I could think of who could advise me or take the reins and save my brother. But I had my friends. I asked my roommate, Gimari, if she and her boyfriend could drive me to Baltimore that night. I called up our childhood neighbor, Selma, and asked to borrow the thousand dollars (which might as well have been a million as far as our family was concerned) that had been set as his bail. My friends, who were as young and powerless as I was, all understood the desperately high stakes of the situation. They readily agreed to help in whatever way they could.

I started crying as soon as we got into the car, and I don't think I stopped until we reached the police station. Baltimore seemed desolate to me that night, like its spirit had been broken. Through my tears, I imagined that those empty city streets had nothing to offer me but a terrible ending.

I had worked so hard trying to avoid this exact situation. I had planned for and lectured to and watched over my brother so very carefully, and apparently, none of that had mattered in the end. It didn't matter what he wore or how polite he was, if he was a college student or a kid on a street corner. Respectability had made no difference. It felt like a walking nightmare; Maurice had ended up in the place that terrified me the most. This one mistake could ruin every-thing for my brother and my family. It could break our hearts in a way that we would never recover from. It had caused a chasm in the very earth I stood on. I knew what it meant when a young Black man got caught in the prison industrial complex. I understood that there was rarely, if ever, a second chance. I was terrified that my sweet, beloved little brother might be facing something that would destroy his whole life.

I started to cry again when they brought him out from his jail cell. It was the way his voice trembled when he said my name, the vulnerable look on his face; he was so scared. He looked like he was five years old all over again. I folded him into my arms and wept, relieved to see that he was okay, that he wasn't hurt. The image of Rodney King's battered face had been filling my mind the whole drive down. I pulled back and gently touched Maurice's cheek, his forehead, his hair.

I took his arm and led him to the car, and then, as anger replaced relief, I roundly cursed him out. *How the fuck could he be so stupid? What the hell had he gotten himself into? Did he know just how fucking bad this could be?*

Maurice explained that he had been hanging out with some upperclassmen at school who had been breaking into dorm rooms and stealing valuables, then taking them to local pawn shops. He swore he hadn't been part of the fenc-ing, but they were his friends, and when they had asked him if they could use his student identification at the pawn shop because—for one contrived reason or another—their identification wouldn't work, Maurice had fallen back into his old pattern of wanting to please, to be liked, and apparently offered it up without hesitation.

I felt like shaking him. "So the stolen stuff was traced back to you," I said.

"They're good guys!" he answered. "I'm sure they didn't know this would happen." Then his face changed, and he looked unsure. "Did they?"

I closed my eyes. I couldn't look at him. "You are going to give the police every one of their names."

He sounded alarmed. "I can't—I can't do that! They'll know!"

I gripped his arm. "And it won't matter because you are withdrawing from that school and will never see them again. You're coming back home tonight. You're going to enroll at Howard next semester, and we will find a way to fix this. I swear we will."

He didn't argue.

As we drove through the night, his head resting on my shoulder as he slept, I reflected on the fact that, except for that brief moment just after his call, I hadn't fallen back on my usual wish for a magical parental figure who could fix things for us. Instead, I'd thought, *Maurice and I will handle this together. We will have the courage to face this, and we will learn from our mistakes, and then we will move forward.*

It was, as always, me and my brother against the world.

I just hoped that would be enough.

———

I STARTED WRITING LAWYERS AS SOON AS WE ARRIVED home. I knew that Maurice would need someone better than some overburdened state-appointed public defender. But I also knew that we had no money to pay anyone. As luck would have it, I happened to be taking a prelaw class at the time, and my professor, a big, muscular man who I might have mistaken for a football player, was happy to help me draft the letter I planned to send out to a dozen different defense lawyers.

He peered down through his reading glasses at my first clumsily written attempt. "What you need to ask is if they are willing to work pro bono," he said, once again giving me a vocabulary I didn't even know existed.

But, of course, most lawyers do not work pro bono. I must have written to more than ten different attorneys, people I had found while doing late-night Google searches: *Best defense lawyers in Maryland. Good lawyers who work for free.* Most didn't even bother to write me back, and those who did only did so to tell me sorry, no, they couldn't be of service.

I do not think it was a coincidence that the one Black lawyer I contacted was the person who finally stepped forward to help.

When I think of John Smith, I think of this Baldwin quotation: "I am very much concerned that American Negroes achieve their freedom here in the United States. But I am also concerned for their dignity, for the health of their souls, and must oppose any attempt that Negroes may make to do to others what has been done to them."

I think John Smith cared about the dignity and health of

my family's soul. I think that's why he took my brother's case. He wanted our family to recover. He was willing to fight for Maurice to be one of the very few Black men who get a second chance in our system. He wanted Maurice, and our family, to come out of this awful experience intact.

I remember meeting him and immediately feeling this immense relief. I knew this man would get us through. He was tall, with a very thin frame, but he wore a big, colorful suit. It was so oversized and stylish that it almost reminded me of something from the Harlem Renaissance. He had glasses and curly hair and just exuded this confidence and pride. It seemed to me that he had probably gone through some hard things to get where he was at, and because of that, he could understand our family. He was filled with determination and integrity, and he saw Maurice and our little family as having value, as being worthy of protection.

John Smith got the charges dismissed on a technicality. Then he got Maurice's record expunged, so that there was no chance of any of this coming back to hurt him later.

Maurice finished school at Howard and became an incredible teacher. He is still sweet and funny, a good-hearted man who is invested in the larger community. If he changed because of this experience, it was only for the better; he is still a charmer and a kind person, but he can stand on his own. He doesn't people please anymore. And these days? He sometimes takes care of me.

He is still my best friend. And I still worry over his right to merely exist in this world.

I know how lucky we were. I know that most Black boys

or men who find themselves swept into the system don't ever make it out. That most Black people in America who make a mistake like Maurice did don't get a second chance. We were lucky that he wasn't beaten, that he wasn't killed, that he wasn't incarcerated and stuck inside a system that *intended for him to perish*. And, of course, it's no longer just Rodney King's name that I carry with me, but George, Freddie, Tamir (who looked so much like a young Maurice that I burst into tears when I saw his face), Sandra, Daunte, Breonna, Elijah, Philando, Eric, Trayvon, Amadou, Emmett . . . There is barely enough breath left in my body to say all the names of those who are gone.

They all should have had our luck, been given the same chance for a new beginning. They should have been allowed to exist on this earth without fear. Our family was not particularly special. I would bet you anything that every person whose name I just wrote down had people who loved them and tried their best to protect them, and intimately knew the helpless feeling of trying to shelter someone from what felt like an inevitable, heartbreaking end.

I think often of the final words in Baldwin's essay to his nephew:

> *God gave Noah the rainbow sign, No more water, the fire next time!*

Baldwin's words chill me because I know that he is right. It will be a fire next time. Years later, I watched police officers dressed in full riot gear outside my apartment in Los Angeles. Body armor. Helmets. Batons. People filled the streets and held posters that read BLACK LIVES MATTER and SAY HER NAME. My son was only two months old when I joined the moving crowd of protesters. I could feel the heaviness of our rage and collective grief. In unison, we chanted, *"No justice, No peace,"* demanding accountability for another Black person killed by the police. Their deaths were not isolated tragedies, but the result of an endless cycle of inequality. Floyd's final words, "I can't breathe," moved millions of people to march and demand police reform. Enough was enough. We can't keep carrying this pain and injustice and fear forever. I have a son who deserves protection. Another valuable, vulnerable Black boy brought into this dangerous world. I don't want this for him. I won't accept it.

And, as a Black woman, I am exhausted, so very tired of fighting, of protecting, of throwing my body between those I love and the precipice that stretches out in front of them. But that doesn't mean I will give up. Baldwin didn't just give me words for my heartbreak and fear. Yes, he testified about our Black pain, the weight we carry, and all the violence we face as a people. But he also regularly evoked radical hope. He gave us answers. He showed us how to have these difficult conversations. He never hesitated to demand the world that we are owed.

And so I return to Baldwin like water from the well. His words, his thoughts, his philosophy—they give me enough cautious optimism that I can look into my brothers' faces, that I can hold my baby boy in my arms, and not fall into an abyss of despair. I will continue to fight, to protect my heart, and protect my space, and protect those I love, and enjoy the way they now sometimes rise to protect me. I will find a little corner of joy for us all, where we can wait for what's to come. Because what other way forward can there ever be? As Baldwin wrote, "If we had not loved each other, none of us would have survived."

CHAPTER NINE

Audre Lorde, *Sister Outsider*

My mother kept everything.

Receipts. Photographs. Old pieces of junk mail. My father had been gone for over a decade, but I had just unearthed his foreign exchange permit application for Howard. It dated back to 1984.

I was crouched over a box on the floor of my bedroom, slowly sifting through years of paperwork that my mother had dragged with us from temporary home to temporary home. The task had felt urgent at first. I was hoping to find something, anything, that would help me understand the silence that had continued to grow in my mother like a tumor, like a debt—the way the night takes over a room in the dead of winter, creeping slowly and then, all at once, you're sitting in the dark. But my search had lost momentum with every useless piece of paper I pulled out and examined. I was looking for insurance receipts or notes from a long-lost doctor, some magical piece of the medical puzzle that would explain to me exactly what was wrong with my mother—how to get her out of bed, how to wipe that slack look from her face, how to make her open her mouth and speak to us once more. But as my hands drifted through those loose pages, all I found was a wash of useless detritus.

I kept digging: a contract for a long-ago apartment lease, over and voided. Maurice's report card from the first grade. My report card from the sixth. *Glory is very bright but she needs to learn to be patient and wait her turn to speak. Maurice has great potential, but he can't seem to sit still and listen.* I rolled my eyes as I tossed those aside. A sepia-toned photograph of a smiling couple I didn't recognize, in front of a house I had never seen before, obviously in Nigeria. I flipped the photo over, hoping for a written explanation on the back, but it was blank.

I sighed and cracked my neck, sore from sitting in one place for too long. It was getting late. If I didn't go to bed soon, I knew I'd hate myself the next morning when my alarm went off at five A.M. and the endless day stretched in front of me. I had to guide my mother from her bed, watch her as she brushed her teeth and washed her face before she turned around and shuffled back under the quilt again. I had to bring her a cup of tea, a slice of toast, an apple or banana, and then wait patiently to make sure she actually ate at least part of it. I had to discuss the day's plans with Maurice, find out when he would return home and if he could stop at the store or maybe even pick up Tunde from school, or whether those jobs would be mine to complete. I had my own classes to attend, a tutoring session to run, the daily challenge of pretending to be an average, happy, functional senior in college, not a desperate, exhausted caretaker, sister, and daughter who could barely keep the lights on and spent her nights looking for a miracle in a dusty cardboard box.

I yawned. There was more to look through, but I was done for the night. I gathered up the papers I'd already sorted and tried to shove them upright into one side of the box, hoping to leave myself with some sort of order when I returned to the task, but as I reached deeper to make room, my hand bumped up against something at the cardboard bottom.

A packet of envelopes. Neatly bound together with a green string. I glanced at the post stamp. Letters from Nigeria. I lifted them from the box and squinted, looking closer, and I felt my heart contract in my chest. There was my name, *Miss Glory Edim*, written across the front of the envelope in what I immediately recognized as my father's flowing script.

I pulled the top letter from the packet. The envelope hadn't even been opened.

I quickly shook out the rest of the letters. Maybe three dozen in all, some addressed to me, some addressed to Maurice, a few of them opened, but the rest were sealed, unread. All from my father. Three or four sent every year since he left us, the year I turned twelve and thought I had lost him for good.

I opened the first envelope with trembling hands. He had written it when I was sixteen years old.

My Princess, I read, and a rush of hot tears clogged my

throat, remembering how my father had called me this pet name. I was always his princess and Maurice had been his champ.

> My Princess,
> It has been almost four years since I last saw you and your brother. I pray to God daily to guide and protect your lives till we meet again soon.

Five pages. Five pages of my father's words, his thoughts, his affection. All just for me. It was like I had been freezing to death and managed to somehow unearth a piece of the sun.

> Please bear with me. I have not neglected both of you. You are all always in my mind and prayers every single day. . . . It is very painful when I set to reflect on how and why my marriage to your mother broke up. . . . I know I am a good father and loved your mother so much. The question is, what went wrong? Who is to blame?

Even before she became ill, my mother had refused to answer my questions about my father or their marriage. She rarely spoke of the past at all, changing the subject with such firm alacrity, in such a charming way, that I knew there was no hope in pursuing it. When I asked her to describe Creek Town, her birthplace in Nigeria, she smiled, saying, "Let me think," and then suddenly complimented the gap in my smile. Throughout my childhood she pleasantly avoided any

inquiries about her upbringing. Instead she wrote nonde-
script notes, reminders, and biblical scriptures to herself. I'd
find scraps of paper in the kitchen with questions like, "What
year did your brother die?"

I knew they were unanswered aspects of her past life, one
where we didn't exist and her unnamed brother did.

When my mother lost her voice, I wondered if it was the
result of all her secrets compounded, heavy in her throat.

> I love both of you so much and you two mean the whole
> world to me. I know in your heart you will forgive me for
> not being there for you, and I pray, no matter how long, I
> will be able to make up for my absence.

I leaned back on my heels, tenderly stroking the paper
with my fingertips, mesmerized by the fact that after all
these years, a path back to my father had been opened up,
just when I needed it most.

> I hope this arrives before your birthday. By the way, my
> birthday is the day before yours.

I swallowed hard, thinking of him faithfully sending the
letters all these years. Imagining my mother fetching them
from the mailbox and then promptly hiding them from us,
unread and unacknowledged. I felt robbed. It was time I
could never get back.

I imagined marching out of my room, letters in hand,
shaking my mother awake, throwing them into her lap, de-

manding she tell me *why*. I felt a sickening slide of rage in my gut as I realized that I couldn't ever confront my mother about this betrayal. It was too risky. She was too fragile. And, of course, even if she had been stronger, she no longer had a voice with which she could explain herself.

I pictured my father, struggling to make a life in Nigeria, waiting for a response from his children that never came. I thought I'd been abandoned, that he simply didn't care. After he left and I didn't hear from him again, I had taken my mother's side and blamed him for everything. But for the first twelve years of my life, my father had been my dearest friend, my fondest reflection, the one who understood me the best of all.

How could he think I would ever forget our birthdays were a day apart?

He must have worried that we had erased him. He must have felt as abandoned by me as I'd felt by him.

I wish you all the best life has to offer with all of my heart.
Please write.

A few months after I found the letters, a relative called to tell me that my maternal grandmother had passed away.

I didn't know what to do.

I knew what I was *supposed* to do. All the relatives who called me from Nigeria—people I hardly knew and hadn't seen face-to-face for years—made sure I understood my duties. I was supposed to find a way for my mother to return home so she could arrange a proper burial. A daughter needs to see that her mother is buried correctly. And if I couldn't do that (but what kind of ungrateful monster of a child wouldn't do that?), at the very least, I was supposed to send money so that someone else could take care of the arrangements. And, obviously, the first thing I was supposed to do was break the news to my mother that her mother no longer walked this earth.

But I couldn't do any of those things. There was no money to send. No question of us traveling when my mom could barely stagger from her bed to the bathroom. And I instinctually knew that if I told my mother that her mother was gone, she would free fall into a pit so deep, she might never return.

I had worked endlessly to keep things under control for all these years. I'd raised my brothers and cared for my mother and kept our secrets from the world. I'd been so doggedly protective of our hidden life that I'd dated a boy for two years who knew absolutely nothing about my family or home. To him, I was just a pretty, uncomplicated college girl who liked to go out dancing, reliably laughed at his jokes, and never, ever invited him back to her place.

But the weight of this secret felt different. Even though most of the time my mother seemed to be drifting elsewhere, she was quite literally still there. She was still in the house, still an observer to everything that happened under our roof, even if she wasn't directly participating. Sometimes I would turn and find her eyes on me—they seemed to grow bigger each day as her face slowly grew thinner due to her lack of appetite—and I became convinced that she knew I was hiding something from her. That she could tell.

I was worn to the bone, juggling my final year of college, a full-time job, caring for both brothers (though Maurice had started to step up and contribute as he could), and still trying my best to get my mother the help she needed. We had moved into our own apartment by then, but we had no health insurance, no savings, and the money that Maurice and I pooled just barely covered food, rent, and utilities each month. There was absolutely nothing extra, and it was becoming clear to me that my mother might not ever get better. She might spend the rest of her life in her bed, eyes growing bigger and bigger, as she drifted off into her small, voiceless world. And I would have to find a way to care for her for as long as she might need me.

It had always felt difficult, but now, compounded with the secret of my grandmother's death, it started to feel nearly impossible. It left me wide-awake at night, heart beating out of my chest, as my brain cycled and re-cycled through all the most terrible possibilities and scenarios. It left me longing for relief, for connection, for someone to love me enough to lift my burdens—even if it was just for a moment.

My mother was lost to me.

I needed to find my father.

So I did what Nigerians do when we need to find someone. I reached out to everyone I knew in our small community in the United States and told them that I was looking for him. "If you're going back home, can you try to find my dad? Can you tell him what's going on? Can you send word?"

It was shockingly easy and quick. It didn't take long at all for a family friend, our Uncle Chris, to reach him. As it turned out, my father had also been looking for us for years with no luck. We'd been so transient, and my mother hadn't bothered to send him any updated information. We had been as invisible to him as he was to us.

Uncle Chris came back from Nigeria and told me, "Your dad is doing really well." He had built a house in his village, and he was working for the Nigerian government doing urban planning. He had remarried and had two teenage stepdaughters, and he wanted me to come visit. He said he'd buy the ticket and help me get my visa. Uncle Chris gave me his email.

It was arranged in a matter of weeks. I would go home for Christmas vacation. (It didn't matter where I had been born, where we actually lived, or how long it had been since we had returned; Nigeria was always referred to as home.) My father wrote that he couldn't wait to see me.

I didn't tell my mother where I was going. I was still so angry with her for keeping the letters from us, and even in her weakened and helpless state, I didn't trust her. I couldn't help but think that, if she knew, she might somehow manage to stop me from seeing my father again.

I HAD TWELVE UNINTERRUPTED HOURS ON THE PLANE, A rare treat. I honestly couldn't remember ever having an entire twelve hours to myself before, and I was determined to take full advantage and read for the entire flight. I would have liked to have started a new book, but that would mean I'd have to spend the money to buy it, and that wasn't really an option, so I went to my own bookshelf to pick something out. I ran my finger down a few different spines, considering my choices. I could read something light and charming, purely for pleasure. Or I could read something assigned for school, getting ahead of my work. I could reread something for comfort and nostalgia, something I already knew and loved and understood.

Sister Outsider by Audre Lorde was none of the above. My hand paused on the paperback, and it felt like a little bell rang inside my head. The title spoke to me; I could answer to both those names.

I'd already read this collection of essays and speeches in one of my African American literature classes a couple of years earlier. I understood the book's importance. I knew that Lorde was a queer Black writer, a pioneer of intersectional feminism, and had been at the forefront of the Black Radical tradition. I'd read and loved her poetry as well. But while I was in school and also caring for my family, I could only allow myself the time to read things at a surface level. I read to write the papers, to take the tests, to pass my classes. Deep study—the luxury of actually sitting with a complicated text for more than a minute—was an extravagance I simply couldn't afford. *Sister Outsider* was a rich and complex book, and I knew that I hadn't given Lorde's essays the time they needed to truly absorb their depth.

I remembered also that Lorde had been a librarian before she became a full-time writer, and I had recently been toying with the idea of doing my graduate work in library science. I'd studied journalism and loved it, and I almost had my degree, but I didn't know how that was going to translate into a real job. When I started at Howard, in that first year before my family had come to live with me, I'd been very free-spirited about my career choices. I saw myself as a creative, someone with unlimited options. But now it was looking more and more likely that I would have to take care of my mom for the rest of her life, and that translated into me turning my back on any kind of risky freelance employment in the arts. I decided that it would be selfish to try to find and follow a passion. I just needed stability. Maybe I'd work at a school, or a library. Someplace with insurance and regular hours and paid time off. Someplace where I could depend on a decent check being handed to me every two weeks. The fact that Audre Lorde was a divorced mother and had that kind of job before she became a full-time writer spoke to me as well. She made me hopeful. Here was a woman who managed to be great, to contribute the deepest and most radical kind of thought to the world, while still paying her own bills and taking care of her family.

I pulled the book from the shelf and looked at the cover. I slid it carefully into my backpack.

MY PLAN FOR A LUXURIOUS DEEP READ ON THE PLANE WAS immediately disrupted by the extremely handsome and friendly young man who sat down next to me. I remember his beautiful face, but I wish I could remember his name. He started a conversation with me at once, not even giving me a chance to crack open the book I had been waiting so impatiently to immerse myself in. But I'd be lying if I didn't admit that my annoyance was tempered by his ridiculously attractive smile.

He, too, was traveling back home for Christmas Carnival. Most of the people on the plane that day were probably doing the same thing. It is customary for everyone in the West and Europe to head back home at that time of year. He was first generation like me, but he had been home at least yearly for the holidays since he was a child, and I remember being startled by the depth of his knowledge.

He told me about his family, where he was from, and he rhapsodized about all the cooking and prepping they would be doing for the holiday. He told me about the township his parents had been born in, how they had met and courted. He spoke casually and joyously about his tribe, his language, and his culture. He was so familiar with all the small details of his home life.

Then he started asking me questions.

"What area is your tribe from?"

I knew the names of the towns my parents grew up in. I knew that my mother was from Creek Town and my father from Calabar, but I didn't know where, exactly, my tribe was centered.

"Ah! So you must speak Efik!"

He said something in what should have been my native language. The language I barely knew at all.

I shrugged helplessly, feeling my face start to burn, and he laughed in a good-natured way.

"It'll be good for you to go home. You will remember where you are from."

Ever since I was a young child, I've known my identity was cloaked in duality and displacement—the place of my ancestry at odds with the location of my birth. I knew that Calabar was the first capital of Nigeria during British colonial rule before it was moved to Lagos in 1906, then finally relocated to Abuja in 1991, because my father had insisted I memorize this fact. It was an odd point of pride. In his estimation, our homeland was the pinnacle, and he had been the one in our family who fought to keep our culture alive. He made sure that we returned to Nigeria regularly, attended Nigerian events in the United States, and spent time with other Nigerian families. He talked about home all the time. He was so proud of being Nigerian, and he wanted Maurice and me to feel the same way.

My mother had been different. Her appearance was more ambiguous. She was mixed race, and fair-skinned, and had different hair texture than my father. People often thought she was Hispanic, and most of the time she didn't bother to correct them. If we got into a cab and the driver was Nigerian, my father would immediately become his best friend, but my mother would ignore the coincidence. She said she believed in assimilation, but sometimes I thought that what she really believed in was reinvention: leaving her past self firmly behind.

After my father left, we stopped traveling back home. Our family connection to Nigeria grew weaker. Holding on to our homeland became secondary to surviving in our adopted country.

And now this man was asking me questions I could not

answer, and even though he was perfectly nice about my stuttering hesitation and uncomfortable shrugs, I felt a sharp mix of shame and envy. I wanted to participate in the conversation in a way that didn't make me feel so inadequate. I felt less and less Nigerian as he spoke to me. This handsome stranger knew so much, and I knew so little.

I finally, abruptly, told him that I needed to read my book for school. A small lie, but his questions were making my heart speed up and my throat dry. I already carried that little girl inside me who had been left so young, the child who secretly blamed herself for her father's absence. I was half convinced that my parents' marriage had ended because of something I had or had not done. That same uncertain part of me thought that my mother's illness was surely my fault as well. I couldn't help but worry that when I was finally reunited with my father, he might still be angry with me for those mistakes.

It didn't make any sense, really. My father was a mild-tempered man. When my parents were still together, he'd always been the fun parent with the soft touch. He'd let my mom do all the labor, take care of all the discipline, and then he'd sweep in and console us, wipe our tears, and distract us with a game or a sweet treat. There was no reason for me to think he would be angry or would lash out at me in any way. But when someone survives trauma, they can't help but see danger in every possibility.

And now, on top of those fears, I was suddenly scared that I wouldn't be Nigerian enough for my father, either. That I would embarrass and disappoint him.

I crawled into my book like it was a bed, hoping that Audre Lorde's words would loosen the tight feeling in my chest and dim the anxious voices chattering in my brain.

THERE IS SOMETHING MAGICAL ABOUT FINDING JUST THE right book at just the right time. It has happened to me over and over, and it never feels like a coincidence. It feels like fate or grace. If I believed in angels, my seraphim would speak to me through printed words on a page.

The first couple of chapters were interesting, but I paused for a moment when I saw the title of the third chapter in the book, a speech Lorde gave to the Modern Language Association: "The Transformation of Silence into Language and Action." That title summed up exactly what I wanted more than anything else in the world. My hands began to gently tingle, as they sometimes do when I start to read something that just might change everything.

The first line of the speech made me reach for my pen and begin to frantically underline: "I have come to believe over and over again that what is most important to me must be spoken, made verbal and shared, even at the risk of having it bruised or misunderstood."

Our family was built upon secrets, bound by silence. Things that went unsaid were so much more than polite pauses in our conversations; those negative spaces had grown so large and powerful, they had *become* my life. The idea that someone was insisting that those missing words must be "verbal and shared," no matter the consequences, felt like revelatory relief.

The famous line "Your silence will not protect you" came from this text, and when I reached those words — "My silence had not protected me. Your silence will not protect you." — I sucked in my breath. It felt so personal. I viscerally understood what Lorde was saying in a way that I hadn't the first time I read it through.

Lorde went on to write about how unexpressed words could become your core, that they would decay you from within. She was handing me the rarest kind of offering: companionship in my thoughts and fears, an acknowledgment that I was not alone. I saw that particular truth, that decay, play itself out on a daily basis. My mother's muteness was rooted in refusal. She was angry and scared, hiding letters and keeping secrets, to the point where she had run out of even the simplest of words.

I was petrified I would become her. I had always wondered if her illness was genetic, if one day I would be doomed to follow her into the bed, into that same dark, silent world. But Lorde allowed me to consider the idea that maybe the real reason my mother was ill was because she had built up so much resentment, she had become incapacitated, choking on her own pain.

It was suddenly clear to me; my mother was drowning in secrets and anger and silence, and by following her example, I was throwing myself into the same sea.

I closed the book for a moment, stunned to have it laid out so plainly. This was the truth I had been searching for as I had pawed through that cardboard box. The answers had been sitting quietly behind me on my bookshelf, just waiting to be found.

But even if I now had an idea about *why* my mother was the way she was, even if I recognized that I was stumbling down the path she had blazed before me, I still didn't know *how* to veer off from that particular journey.

I glanced over at the handsome man. He was sleeping now, his mouth hanging open and his head lolling to one side. I allowed myself to watch him for a moment, wondering how he could be comfortable enough to let down his guard even while surrounded by strangers.

I sighed and then opened the book again, certain that Lorde would have more to say to me.

"The deepest understructure of which was Hatred, that societal death wish directed against us from the moment we were born Black and female in America," I read.

One of the main premises of the essay "Eye to Eye: Black Women, Hatred, and Anger" is that Black women in America are immersed in such strong hatred and racism from the moment that they entered this world that they cannot help but turn this hatred and anger onto other Black women who they see as a mirror, reflecting back that degraded part of themselves.

I recognized something of the truth in this idea, but from a bit of a distance. Because both of my parents were Nigerian and I was first generation, even understanding the history of segregation and Jim Crow laws was not always easy, nor was assessing how that history influenced the way people saw me and how I showed up in the world. This is not to say that I didn't experience the kind of virulent racism and sexism that Lorde described. Of course I did—I had grown up as a Black girl in America, and there was no escaping the unending indignities and outright brutality attached to that. "Growing up, metabolizing hatred like a daily bread," Lorde wrote. But this friction between peers that Lorde talked about didn't apply to me personally. I was lucky to have had incredibly fortifying relationships with my Black women friends. Sometimes it felt as if the women I knew in college were the only thing keeping me in the light. But when I gave just the smallest twist to the dial of this idea, I realized that I could apply what she was saying to my relationship with my mother, and to my mother's relationship to her own self and sanity.

My mother acted as my dreaded mirror, and perhaps her withdrawal from the world was born of a desperate reluctance to gaze too closely on her own battered reflection.

"My mother," wrote Lorde, "was a very brave woman, born in the West Indies, unprepared for America. And she disarms me with her silences."

The hairs on the back of my neck crept up as I read those words.

"My mother taught me to survive from a very early age by her own example. Her silences also taught me isolation, mistrust, self-rejection and sadness."

Here again, it felt as if Lorde was scooping the thoughts straight from the jumble in my head and handing them back to me re-formed, neatly ordered, and gleaming with wisdom.

"And survival is the greatest gift of love. Sometimes, for Black mothers, it is the only gift possible and tenderness gets lost."

This had been true when I was younger, before my

mother had become ill. Our relationship had been complicated. My mother had not always approved of me, but she
had made sure to teach me the things she felt were vital for
me to exist in our society. She had paid attention and had
opinions and wanted certain outcomes for me. And, know-
ingly or not, she had given me access to the creative flow.
Because of her working the night shift, I had always cared for
my brothers, but, at least when she was home and awake, I'd
been allowed a measure of precious uninterrupted time. A
chance to think and read and daydream and drift away from
my body without the burden of survival bullying its way
into my brain and pulling me back into reality every chance
it got. I'd been allowed an interior life, something that had
been necessarily sacrificed after she became ill.

To me, there is an ideal, incremental way to grow apart
from your mother. You go through adolescence and develop
your independence and a sense of rebelliousness, and there is
a push and pull that eventually allows for a mutual and
healthy separation. You go away, and then maybe you come
back, and then you go away again. You stand mainly on your
own, with the comforting thought that your mother is always somewhere in the background, willing to step forward
and catch you with a steadying hand if you should need it.

There is also an ideal path to lose your parents in a more
permanent way. You grow up and build your own life and
family apart from them. You become dependent on the support of a partner and children or your chosen family. You
mature as your parents age. They weaken, and you care for
them until it is time to let go.

As Lorde puts it, "All mothers see their daughters leaving. . . . All daughters see their mothers leaving." Every step on that road allows you to prepare for that loss.

But I wasn't given the luxury of that preparation. My father disappeared to another continent pretty much overnight. My mother left almost as abruptly, even if she physically stayed within my proximity. And so, Lorde's words made my breath catch in my throat again and again.

As I read those words, I realized that I no longer had a mother.

Even though she was physically present, the mental and emotional support that I needed to thrive, to be the person I wanted to be, simply wasn't there anymore. Even the basic maternal impulse that she used to feel, the impulse to aid in my survival, had disappeared.

Her illness had taken her from me.

Again I shut the book, this time so I could rise to my feet, slide past my seatmate, make my way down to the restroom, and sit in that pathetic and solitary space, sobbing silently into my fists as we continued to hurtle through the sky.

MY HANDSOME FRIEND CAME THROUGH FOR ME AGAIN once we arrived at the airport. The last time I had been overseas, I'd been a small child with my parents leading the way. As soon as I stepped off the plane, I realized I had no idea how to navigate the red tape that would allow me to leave the airport, that I had no way to reach my father on my now-useless phone, that I didn't know how to gather my luggage or get to the place where we had agreed to meet.

And worst of all, more than a decade had passed since I

had last seen him. *What if he looks different? What if I can't recognize him? What if he can't recognize me? What if I get stuck in this airport forever?*

I had forgotten that there was a certain gruffness, a cultural nuance in Nigeria different from what I knew in the United States. There was no such thing as customer service as I understood it. No Nigerian made their living patiently smiling at you and metaphorically holding your hand—you had to be prepared and aggressive and ready to boldly state what you wanted. But I was drained and emotional and flustered and obviously very American. I immediately attracted a dozen different people who either wanted something from me or wanted me to want something from them.

My seatmate must have seen me looking dazed and miserable, because he doubled back and touched my arm.

"Can I help you through?" he said.

The relief I felt was the strangest sort of novelty. I'd been responsible for myself for so very long; I'd grown used to extricating myself from difficult situations, bluffing my way through things, protecting myself at every turn.

I looked at him and nodded. "Thank you" was all I could muster as he took my arm and led me down the corridor. Through customs and baggage claim, through purchasing a SIM card and installing it in my phone, and then finally, through navigating to the waiting area, where, after me giving a cheerful salute, he set off on his way.

I turned to watch him leave, feeling ridiculously bereft, the confidence his presence had given me draining away with every step he took.

I shook my head, disgusted. *Pull your shit together,* I commanded myself. I forced a deep breath, and I turned around.

And he was there.

He was just . . . there. My father. Just like he said he would be.

And it was like no time had passed, and all of the things that had happened didn't matter. He held out his arms as he sort of stumbled toward me, halfway to running. I laughed and rushed toward him, and then I was wrapped up in his hug, and he smelled the same and he felt the same and it was as if everything was exactly the same as it had been ten years before—before he left, before my mother disappeared, before the weight of our small world had been laid entirely upon my shoulders.

"My princess," he said, placing a kiss on the crown of my head.

That's when I started to cry because, more than anything, his voice (his voice!) was exactly the same. Familiar and sweet and comforting. And as he murmured endearments and gave me another fond kiss, I felt that immense weight I had been carrying slide away from me like rain pouring off the slant of a roof.

I was somebody's child once more.

TAKING INSPIRATION FROM *SISTER OUTSIDER*, I'D EVENTU-ally washed my face and left the restroom on the plane, sat back in my seat, and made a plan. I decided that I would be bold and fearless and say all the things to my father that I'd been saving up for years. I was so sick of the secrets. The book had given me a map for how I wanted to be once I was in Nigeria. It gave me language and a frame for what needed to be said. I wanted to confront him. I wanted to tell him that I loved him but also that I was angry at him. That I was disappointed. I had stories to tell and questions to ask. His letters had given me some relief, but there was so much more that I needed to express. I wanted him to know exactly what was going on with my mother. He needed to know what Maurice and I had been through, what we had given up, what his absence had cost us.

I also imagined the relief I would feel dumping all my problems into my father's lap, letting him sort them all out for me. I thought that this visit was my chance to change everything. There was so much that needed to be fixed, and I only had two weeks before I would go back to D.C. I promised myself I would not let the things I needed to say wait.

But on the ride back from the airport, I was too giddy to talk about any of that. I was lost in the sheer pleasure of being a kid again. A kid with a functioning and attentive parent.

My dad seemed equally filled with emotion. He kept reaching over to me as we drove, patting my shoulder or my knee, resting his hand against my cheek, as if he wanted to make sure I was actually there.

"I thought you and your brother didn't want a relationship with me." His voice was filled with wonder. "I thought I'd never see you again."

I couldn't even find the words to answer that, except to grab his hand with my own and squeeze.

———

STEPPING INTO MY FATHER'S HOUSE FOR THE FIRST TIME made me a little dizzy. When I look at pictures of it now, I can see it is just a normal-sized house, but back then, after living in cramped apartments for most of my life, it seemed indescribably grand and massive. It was a gated compound off a single-lane dirt road. The house sat on top of a steep hill with a view of the small township spread below. There was a long veranda out front, scattered with chairs that he later told me he had designed himself. There was a big metal door for extra security.

My father had designed and built this house with his own hands. He had studied both architecture and urban planning at Howard, and the plan had always been that he and my mother would return to Nigeria after he got his degree. That he would create this dream home for her, for me and Maurice, and for my parents' extended family.

But now my mother was no longer his wife, and her mother was dead, and—I realized as he opened up the front door with a proud flourish—he had built this house not for my mother or Maurice and me but for some other woman and her children. Strangers.

Still, when I walked into the foyer and saw all the beautiful African artwork and the good, strong light slanting in from the windows in the dining room and my father's degree from Howard framed and hung up in pride of place, it felt like it could be mine, too. It felt like a home. I was at once proud and wistful, like I could belong there, but only if we could pick up the whole place and set it back down in D.C.

My father's new wife and her two pretty teenage daughters came out from the kitchen to greet us. The girls beamed at me, shy and sweet, but my stepmother raised her eyebrows and gave me a perfunctory smile that didn't make it all the way to her eyes.

"This is my daughter, Glory," said my dad, throwing his arm over my shoulder.

I should have expected tension. After all, why would this new wife be pleased about the attention my father was giving me, or be accepting of the possibility that my mentally ill mother might somehow ride my coattails back into his life? But I was young and naïve, so I guess I just assumed I would be embraced. Judging from the way my stepmother was looking at me, that was not going to be happening anytime soon.

"Hello, Glory," she said stiffly. "Nice to meet you. The girls and I were just finishing up making dinner. Perhaps you'd like to come in and give us a hand?"

My father waved his arm in dismissal. "Don't be silly!" he boomed. "Glory doesn't have to do any of that stuff! She is our guest!"

I didn't know how to feel about him saying this. On one hand, I could see the anger flare in my stepmother's eyes when he indulged me in this way. Even though I had not grown up in what anyone would call a traditional Nigerian household, living with my stepfather's strictness had taught me enough to know that, as the eldest daughter, I was supposed to be submissive. I was supposed to help in the kitchen and listen to my stepmother and serve my father. I was supposed to show respect.

But on the other hand, I didn't *want* to go help in the kitchen. I knew I'd just be showing them how much I didn't know about cooking, especially traditional Nigerian food. And more importantly, my father certainly wasn't going to be in there with me.

The only thing I was really interested in at that moment was spending as much time with him as possible.

I had felt unloved for a very long time. There had been no room for love back home in D.C.—at least, not the kind of love that wasn't tied up in complicated things like survival and responsibility. I told my brothers that I loved them all the time—I didn't want them to feel the way I did—and they parroted it back at me, but there was no one in my life who ever said it to me first. I was starved for affection, and here was my father, offering up what already felt like huge quantities of the very thing I was so hungry for. No way was I capable of passing that up.

There was a long moment, a standoff, while my step-mother waited to see what I would do. I kept my mouth shut, pretending that I didn't understand just how much etiquette I was ignoring. Finally, she frowned and shook her head.

"Fine," she snapped, turning her back on us and heading into the kitchen.

The girls stared at us, wide-eyed at the rebellion that my father had encouraged, but then hurried back into the kitchen when their mother called their names.

"How long before dinner is ready?" my father called after them.

"Not long," my stepmother answered back.

My father winked at me. "That sounds like long enough to go get a beer and watch some football," he whispered.

I knew I was only pouring gasoline on the fire of my stepmother's indignation, but I nodded eagerly as he put his finger to his lips and motioned that we should tiptoe back out the door.

OVER THE NEXT COUPLE OF WEEKS, MY DAD TOOK ME everywhere with him: to the bar, to work, out to eat. It delighted me to see that he was truly beloved and respected in his village. He was friendly with everyone, and everyone adored him in return. They called him the Big Man, the Chief. They laughed at his jokes and slapped him on the back and all but cheered when he came into the room.

And everywhere we went, he introduced me like I was visiting royalty, telling everyone how smart I was, how I was following in his footsteps at Howard, how well I had taken care of my younger brothers and my mother for all these years.

But despite my father's unbridled paternal enthusiasm, the villagers seemed less than impressed with me. The village was tiny—imagine a little country town in North Carolina or Georgia—and I was continuing to ignore all the things an eldest Nigerian daughter was supposed to do. Not only was I not helping out in the house or spending much time with my stepmom and sisters, but I was loud and opinionated. I talked a lot, and I talked back. My father thought I was delightful and uproariously funny. He encouraged me at every turn. But even though I couldn't speak the language, I could tell that people were talking about me and around me, and that nothing they were saying was very kind.

Sometimes my youngest stepsister, Juanita, would clue me in. Juanita adored my father, and she instantly took a liking to me as well, telling me that she, too, hoped to go to Howard someday.

"They are asking where your brother and mother are," she whispered to me as the adults chattered around us, throwing furtive looks my way.

"What else are they saying?" I demanded.

She bit her lip and looked worried. "They are saying that your mother maybe did not raise you right. Maybe because she is sick? That you don't act as a good daughter should."

I rolled my eyes.

Somehow everyone in town knew that something was wrong with my mother, but no one really understood what it was. Nigerians did not talk about mental health. The concept of depression as a disease was completely foreign. "We'll pray on it," they promised me. "We are praying for your mother." Like prayer could stand in for therapy, medication, and enough money to get either or both.

And honestly, when it came to this subject, my father was no better. We still hadn't had that big, important conversation that I had wanted, but I did hint a bit about what we were going through at home, daydreaming that he might immediately declare that he was leaving his new family and coming back to D.C. with me to make it all better.

Instead, his response was to take me by the hand and say,

"Don't worry, princess. We can pray on it together," which made me want to toss my fork across the room.

Something else that I had conveniently forgotten about my father was that he drank. A lot. This had also been true back when he and my mother were still together, though I didn't think it was anything exceptional back then. But as soon as I watched him down a Heineken at the bar that first night, I'd had a rush of memories: empty cans scattered on the kitchen table and the smell of beer on his breath when he kissed me goodnight. I remembered the sleepy, dopey grin that kicked in after his fourth drink, and how tight my mother's mouth would get when he'd stumble and have to grip the table as he made his way across the kitchen to our bathroom. He wasn't a mean drunk; he never put us in a dangerous situation. There was no abuse. But I realized that he had been a functional alcoholic. And apparently that hadn't changed.

With every day that passed, I became more and more aware of his limitations. I loved him desperately, and it was clear that he loved me back. I soaked up all the attention and affection he offered, and just being in his presence again did help me; it was sweet consolation.

But it was not a remedy.

By the time my visit ended, I could see that the dream of my father somehow being able to take all my burdens from me, and allow me to go home and just be a college kid again while he fixed everything, was nothing more than wishful thinking on my part. And I hadn't done much to make things any better. I had ignored my stepmother's displeasure and the villagers' snide comments, and as we drove to the airport, I decided that I wasn't even going to attempt the conversation I had promised myself I would have with him. Because I knew that my time with my dad was running short, I didn't know when I would see him again, and I just couldn't bear the idea that if I confronted any of those things, I might spoil the addictive comfort of being a child (however briefly) with a functional and loving parent.

We both cried at the airport as we hugged goodbye. Dad thanked me for finding him again, for visiting, and he promised he would send me and Maurice money for school and living expenses whenever he could. He told me he knew that what I was going through with my mother wasn't easy, but he also knew that I would keep taking care of things. That I was strong and smart, and that he, and all the people in the village, would be praying for me.

And then, just like that, I was back on the plane, alone.

I opened my book.

In Lorde's 1982 novel, *Zami: A New Spelling of My Name*, she writes: "I have always wanted to be both man and woman, to incorporate the strongest and richest parts of my mother and father within/into me—to share valleys and mountains upon my body the way the earth does in hills and peaks." Lorde's understanding of her parents enlightened my own. I loved their boldness but didn't want to inherit their fear. They provided me with the tools for survival and self-preservation, but also the seeds of self-destruction. I'd spent my whole life putting myself last. I felt untethered and parentless. When Lorde told me that *I* could mother *myself*, it felt like an electric shock. It was a completely new concept to me: *I* could do the work, *I* could do the healing, *I* could make *myself* better. I had been looking so far outside myself for that elixir. I had tried to cure my mother. I had found my lost father. I had traveled all the way to Nigeria and back to seek out someone who could fill this empty, broken part of me. And now I was being told that I could stop searching because, like a good-luck stone in my pocket, I'd been carrying my own remedy all along.

Lorde's radical writing had transformed me. The idea of the mirror image, of being able to look at my faults and not attack myself, of having tenderness and compassion instead? I think that trip to Nigeria was the start of that. And I know that Lorde's words—those dancing, reflective shards that I could see myself in so clearly—showed me my path forward.

THERE IS A SENSE OF PERPETUAL MOVEMENT AND SOUND in Nigeria that feels nonstop and all-encompassing. It's like a constant static surrounds you, *shh shh shh*. It can be beautiful, but it can also be enervating for someone who is not used to it.

Leaving that behind and coming home to D.C. made me feel of two worlds. I was surprised to find that there was a part of me that had missed the muted texture and hushed sounds of the United States. When I walked back into our apartment, I felt myself relax into the familiar. It was mine. I didn't have to compete with anyone. It was my singular space. Home may not have been simple or easy, but it was

still home, and I had made a relationship with my dysfunction.

My mother was sitting on the couch. Apparently it was
one of those rare days when she'd actually left her bed. She
glanced up at me when I walked in, but then looked away
again, that familiar flat expression sliding across her face. I
put my bags down and went to sit next to her. I was determined to start things right, no more secrets.

"Mom," I said, leaning toward her. "I just got back from
Nigeria. I saw Dad."

She turned her head to look at me, and when I saw the
way that her eyes grew huge at my words, I panicked. There
was no doubt that she had understood what I'd just told her.

"It was beautiful, Mom. Of course, people remembered
you and they wanted to know all about Maurice and Tunde.
Oh, and the food! The food was so good! I swear I could eat
jollof rice every day! In fact, I think I did!"

I was babbling. Talking as fast as I could. Doing my best
to wipe that look off her face, make her forget I'd said anything about my father.

"Oh, and do you remember that farm you told me about?
The place where you could get fresh milk? It's been turned
into a—"

"Glory," she said. Her voice sounded as dusty and ephem-
eral as a cobweb.

I froze.

It was the first time she had spoken in years.

"Y-yes?" I stuttered.

She put her hand on my arm. Her eyes were full of hope.

"My mother," she whispered. "Did you see my mother?"

The breath emptied out of me. Of course she wanted her mother. She wanted her mother because she had been suffering. Just like I had wanted my mother as I suffered. Just like any child on this earth wants that comfort. And just like me, she hadn't been able to ask for what she needed. Until now.

For once, I was the one who couldn't speak.

CHAPTER TEN

Jamaica Kincaid, *At the Bottom of the River*

It took me nearly five years and my mother almost dying before I finally figured out how to get help for her.

Most of the time, what I had come to think of as her madness was just part of our life. Wake up, drink a cup of coffee, spend thirty minutes trying to persuade my mother to eat a bite of toast. Get dressed, check in with my brothers, remind my mother that she hadn't bathed in a week and that today would be the day when she would need to get out of bed. Grab my coat, pick up my bag, say goodbye to my mother, tell her that I'd be home again in a few hours, turn and leave without once expecting her to meet my eyes or say anything in return.

My brothers and I lived with an unspoken agreement to keep our crisis to ourselves, as if acknowledging it to the outside world could somehow make it worse. I kept this secret from my boss, my professors, most of my friends. I dated a boy for two years who had no idea that there was a wraith with my mother's name living in my back room, that I carried a weight that sometimes barely left me standing. Sometimes Maurice would dare to have friends over, and their shouts and laughter would invariably send my mother shuffling out of bed, floating through the room like an ill-kempt spirit. The boys would go silent and stare as she grunted and pointed, driven by some instinctual version of hospitality that she could no longer express.

"What the hell was that?" someone would say after she made her eerie circuit and then drifted back into her room.

And Maurice would shrug and make a joke and change the subject.

It was our everyday reality. One that became so horrific and yet so mundane that we learned to accept her illness in the same way we might accept a leaky faucet or a patch of mold growing in the corner of a room—something that didn't necessarily change how we lived day to day, but that we knew would inevitably become a bigger, more dangerous, crisis.

We struggled to act normally, to keep working toward some sort of future, but sometimes things would get so bad that I could no longer live in denial. Sometimes I would wake up in the middle of the night with a gasp, thinking about how big her eyes were, how thin and bony her arms had become, how I could wrap my fingers around her wrists like she was a toddler. I would compulsively count up the meals she had consumed over the last week, two spoonfuls of soup here, a small bite of rice there, five sips of her tea, and realize that there was no surviving what she was putting herself through. She was quite literally starving herself. I could no longer ignore what was happening. I would have to act.

I sometimes wondered if she knew what she was doing or if she was just too lost in the darkness to have an appetite. I knew she was too much of a believer to actually kill herself. She knew that to be a mortal sin. But was it suicide if you simply took a bite or two less every day? If you let yourself wither and shrink until you were as light and dry as a fall leaf, ready to skitter away on the weakest breeze?

She might die. The idea felt like the inevitable conclusion to our nightmare, and though I never wanted to lose the mother who had raised me, I sometimes wondered if this changeling who haunted our house might be better off if she dropped her final tethers and let go. Then, the fact that I had even considered this idea would send me into a guilty, dizzying panic that would propel me to compulsively google and make desperate calls searching for some sort of institutional support. For someone, anyone, who might have a solution.

Then, in my junior year of college, through a constant repetition of this helpless flailing exercise, I finally figured out the magic words. "Is she a danger to herself or others?"

They had asked me this from the beginning. The question was included in almost every conversation I had about my mother. And at first, too ashamed to admit otherwise, I would hasten to say, "No, no. Of course not. She's just ill. She needs help. But she would never . . ." Which always resulted in exactly nothing.

But one day, too exhausted and worried to reassure the

911 operator I had grown desperate enough to call, I let myself say it.

"Yes. Yes. She might kill herself. She is a danger to herself."

And suddenly, evoked by the darkest of words, the urgency that I felt was magically transferred to this stranger, and help was on the way.

MY MOTHER WAS HOSPITALIZED THREE TIMES. ONCE, MY JUnior year of college; once, my senior year, just before my trip to Nigeria; and once, two years after I graduated, when I was twenty-three years old.

Twice, she came back looking better—her face rounder, her cheeks pinker, a certain brightness in her eyes returned. Twice, she was diagnosed and medicated. Twice, we had hope. Twice, she seemed determined to resume her old self. She would go through the motions of normalcy. Eating and grooming herself, taking her medication, maybe even writing out a few words here and there. And twice, she slowly pulled her familiar silence and helplessness back over herself like the smothering, stinking blanket it had become.

"ARE YOU READY TO COME WITH US, MRS. EDIM?"

She stared at them, her mouth working like she was trying to spit out the word *no*, her refusal to stand her only protest. They gently lifted her to her feet. She was too weak to struggle, but she turned and looked at me over her shoulder, and her eyes, which had been nothing but empty for so long, filled with panic and recrimination — twin coals of pain and fear.

I felt tremendous guilt. I knew she was being forced. I knew that she would never voluntarily choose hospitalization. I knew that if she had been able to speak, she would have raged at me for sending her away. She would have insisted I merely pray for her and accept God's will. But I also knew that if I didn't break the silence, say what we all feared out loud, and put our trust into strangers' hands, we would lose her. Irrevocably, completely, and mortally.

I STARTED TO READ JAMAICA KINCAID'S COLLECTION OF short stories *At the Bottom of the River* after the third time my mother was committed. I was sitting in the hospital, waiting to talk to my mother's doctor.

I know that most people do not like hospitals. I'm sure that for most people, the smells and the sounds and the pain are overwhelming. But I didn't mind. For me, hospitals felt like relief. After years of suffering, my mother was finally in the care of people much more competent and knowledgeable than myself: older, wiser people who knew how to coax her to eat, who didn't just see an unsolvable mystery when they looked into her dim eyes, who were able to help her in more than the sporadic and haphazard way my brothers and I could.

And I liked the waiting room. It reminded me of the library, with its hushed and orderly atmosphere. People were muted and exhausted but generally on their best behavior, too wrapped up in their own bubbles of grief or worry to bother anyone else. I never complained about late appointments or doctors who were behind on their schedules. I just sat in my hard plastic chair, content to read while I waited.

The hospital was not a bad place to be, but sitting there reading Kincaid's famous story "Girl" made me ache. The story was written entirely in a mother's voice as she dispensed (not always kind or useful) advice to her daughter: "Wash the white clothes on Monday and put them on the stone heap; wash the color clothes on Tuesday and put them on the clothesline to dry; don't walk barehead in the hot sun; cook pumpkin fritters in very hot sweet oil."

It felt like salt in my already oozing wound to think about all the much-needed advice my mother had not been able to give me over the years. The skillful rapid-fire, run-on, story-long sentence that Kincaid created sounded so much like the mother I had known. The one-way conversation as the mother lectures her daughter on how to live was so familiar. The rhythm of the words reminded me of how we had once lived, with my mother's recipes for life moving us from task to task, hour to hour, day to day. My mother had set the beat that we all danced to, and now that pulse was silent.

Pre-illness, if I had to describe my mother in two words, I would have said *humorous* and *diligent*. My mother was hilarious, with a loud and ready laugh, but her bone-dry, razor-sharp wit had dissolved completely under her illness. My mother had also religiously believed in order. She had a method for everything, and she wasn't shy about insisting that her procedures be followed. At the time, I had, of course, chafed under her meticulousness, but now I missed it almost as much as I missed her laughter and teasing. I even missed the nagging. It had been so long since I'd been given any instruction for work or life. The books were not everything in my life, but at the time they felt like my only guidance. Kincaid's voice sounded certain, and pointed my mind in a new direction. I imagined I was following a map. I would read a story and suddenly feel inspired, which led me to feel hopeful. Being able to capture a sense of hope was essential. I built a personal library that reassured me that my own happiness was possible. Despite my mother's illness and all that surrounded it. For me, reading was reparative. Toni Morrison compelled me to hone in on my vision. Maya Angelou urged me to take more risks. Alice Walker drove me to build something outside of myself. Somehow their intricate stories and astute observations provided me with an unbreakable foundation. They each captured and portrayed the ineffable qualities of Black womanhood. It was a nourishment beyond material need. It's how my soul found healing and purpose.

"MAJOR DEPRESSION DISORDER AND SELECTIVE MUTISM," said the doctor.

I felt a small release between my shoulders. Previous diagnoses had sounded much more frightening: bipolar disorder, severe social anxiety disorder, schizophrenia. Depression was more familiar. I knew other people who suffered from depression.

"She's responding well to the medication," the doctor

went on. "I think another week, and she should be able to return home."

We knew better than to hope this time. We had felt hope before, and it had caused the disappointment to feel even sharper and more violent when it came. Earlier treatments had created tiny sparks of who my mother had been, but those had always been quickly extinguished.

Still, standing in the waiting room, watching the door she would walk through, my brothers and I held our collective breath. *Maybe,* I let myself think. *Maybe this time.*

And then she was there, and she was standing on her own, and her head was held high and she was smiling at us, and I looked into her eyes and saw her. My mother.

She had returned.

SHE WAS BACK. SHE WAS TALKING AND SHE WAS WALKING and she was bossing us around like nothing had ever happened. We walked back into our apartment that night, and she started to clean up the kitchen, keeping up a running monologue about how dirty things were.

"Don't any of you children know how to wash a dish? How long have these cups been in this sink? I know I taught you better than this."

I couldn't do anything but stare at her. I felt like I was dreaming. It was too good to be true.

This was different than the previous two times. Before, there had been some improvement, but she still looked at us like we were on the other side of a window. There had been something that had always felt temporary in her recovery, that warned us not to get too attached. But this time she was just . . . herself. It was as if the last five years had never happened.

"Why are you standing there like a fool, girl? Help me dry these dishes!"

FOR DAYS, MY BROTHERS AND I WALKED ON EGGSHELLS, too scared to say or do anything that might trigger her and cause a relapse. We followed the doctor's instructions and added in the small tasks that would contribute to her staying well. We got her on disability. We took her to her twice-a-week checkups. We made sure she took her medication. Even though she seemed like the woman she'd been previously, old habits die hard. I didn't trust that she could tend to herself just yet.

What we didn't do—what we never did—was talk about what had happened to us in the previous five years. I think I was waiting for my mother to start the conversation. I thought that, if I gave her enough time, she'd just bring it up one day.

"Oh, hey, remember when I was stuck in bed for years on end and I couldn't talk?"

But she never brought it up. And soon it felt too late for anyone to bring it up. We tacitly agreed to pretend that everything was normal and always had been. And suddenly, underneath all the chatter, we were living with a new kind of silence.

She just went about her business and started to get into ours. It must have been so disorienting for her, trying to mother us all again. We had been forced to grow up while she was gone. I had just spent years telling her what to do. I had taken over all the parenting responsibilities for my little brothers. There was a quiet struggle at first: Who should sign Tunde's permission slip? Who should attend the school conferences? Who had the right to tell anyone what to do? I honestly didn't know if I would ever get over the surreal feeling that engulfed me as I watched her bustle around the kitchen or sit at the table, reading her Bible again.

But as she grew stronger, her rhythm gently reemerged. It was slower than it had been before. There were some pauses, some moments where we had to stop and then start again. It was not as loud. But it was still her. And soon, we all learned to follow the slightly more complicated beat of her heart.

MY MOTHER CONTINUED TO GET BETTER. SHE WENT TO AP-pointments and took her medication. A year passed, and we realized that she could live on her own. That we could live on our own. We found her an apartment where she could be comfortable and close to a train. She made it very clear that she didn't like to be overly reliant on us. So, one by one, we children attended college, took on jobs, became independent, and, looking backward over our shoulders, slowly, and very carefully, left her alone to care for herself. Kincaid's words began to feel relatable again: "My mother and I walk through the rooms of her house. Every crack in the floor holds a significant event. . . . We eat from the same bowl, drink from the same cup; when we sleep, our heads rest on the same pillow. As we walk through the rooms, we merge and separate, merge and separate; soon we shall enter the final stage of our evolution."

EIGHT YEARS AFTER MY MOTHER LEFT THE HOSPITAL THE last time, we were at Tunde's college graduation party. My brother had been in the third grade when our mother first got sick, and now he was a man, graduating with a degree in engineering. Everyone was there, all the family friends, the aunties and uncles who had come back into our orbit once my mother had returned from her darkness. The music was loud. The food was delicious. We were eating and drinking and dancing. Everyone was so proud of what my younger brother had accomplished.

I watched my mother as she sat, the queen of our table, smiling and nodding and taking her due. She now had three children who graduated from college. Three children who were all there at her side. But for a moment, I thought about a different graduation, when Tunde was in the eighth grade, and my mother had been too ill to attend. It had just been me and Maurice, clapping and hollering for our brother, trying to make up for the fact that his mother was back home, stuck in bed, stuck in silence.

I thought about all the events that she had missed: the PTA meetings and soccer games and debate tournaments. All those moments where everyone crowds in for a picture. Where glasses are raised in celebration.

Never again, I thought to myself. She would never miss another big moment. She would be there to meet her grand-children. She would see us through our hardships. She would share in every joy and sorrow. She would be there as a wit-ness, a participant, a center to our family.

"Excuse me," my mother said, rising to her feet and tap-ping her glass. "Excuse me."

The room grew quiet as everyone turned her way. My mother smiled, still so beautiful.

"I just wanted to say congratulations to Tunde. And thank you all for coming." She took a deep breath. "You guys all know that for a little while, I was sick. So I also want to say thank you to Glory and Maurice. For standing up and taking care."

And then everyone raised their glasses and she quickly sat back down, and I looked at my brothers and they both looked back at me, and all three of us were crying.

It was the first time she had ever acknowledged those hard, painful years. It was the first time she had accepted that anything—anything at all—had happened.

And maybe it wasn't the grand family counseling session I had once imagined. Maybe I didn't get the chance to tell her my side of the story. Maybe old grievances weren't aired. Maybe it wasn't the healthiest or most functional way to ad-dress the trauma we had all blundered through together. But it was my mother's voice. It was my mother's voice thank-ing us for what we had done. And that? That miracle, that sweetness, that bit of grace, that flicker of light, that gift from God? On that day—in that blessed moment—it was enough.

CHAPTER ELEVEN

Ta-Nehisi Coates, *Between the World and Me*; Naomi
Jackson, *The Star Side of Bird Hill*; Angela Flournoy, *The
Turner House*

I was twenty-eight and living in Brooklyn, in the Bed-Stuy neighborhood (pre-gentrification), on Tompkins Avenue. I was surviving off of hot fried chicken and happy hour at a bar across the street called Peaches. I was working a job I didn't love for a pathetic excuse for a paycheck. And I had never been happier.

All my life, I had dreamed of living in New York City. And all my life, I had wondered if that kind of big dream was out of my reach. When I was little, I didn't think I would ever get the chance to leave our neighborhood in Arlington. When I was older, expecting to care for my mother for the rest of her life, I made my choices based on what was safe and practical. And of course, New York City had nothing to do with either of those things.

But now, my mother was healthy and living independently. Both my brothers were done with school and settled into good jobs. I had renewed my relationship with my father, and we spoke on the phone at least once every couple of weeks. The burdens I had shouldered since I was a little girl had suddenly been lifted. Everyone I loved was safe and secure. It had taken years, but I finally felt that the world and all its possibilities had opened back up to me again.

THE FIRST SIX MONTHS IN THE CITY HAD BEEN AN ADJUST-ment. But after my first lonely birthday in that dusty apartment, the Well-Read Black Girl T-shirt had worked its magic, and New York had started to live up to my sky-high expectations. People were stopping me on the street to ask about the shirt, and those questions almost always progressed into a conversation, and many of those conversations turned into friendships. It was like a fantasy come true. All these fascinating new people in my life—artists and writers and musicians, activists and teachers—all connected to me because we shared a love of books.

I have always been the keeper of my friendships. I gladly take on the job of planning our dinners, scheduling our outings, and organizing retreats with my girlfriends. Maybe because things were difficult at home for so many years, I depended on my friendships for the kind of foundation and support that most people expect from their family. I was constantly thinking of new ways to cultivate those bonds. And I was determined to apply these efforts to all the new people I was meeting as well.

So the Well-Read Black Girl Book Club really started as nothing but a fun way to continue the conversations I was having on the street—to hang out with my friends and talk about books. I did have a background in marketing and branding, but it never occurred to me to apply it to the club. I simply wanted a reason to meet up and read books with other people. I wanted to capture and prolong the feeling I got from talking to these strangers about my T-shirt, and I wanted to share it with my friends, both old and new.

It was never my intention to be an author or have a platform. I did start an Instagram account for Well-Read Black Girl, but it was just a visual diary of my time in New York—things I ate, places I went, or books I read. The pictures were low quality; there was no grandiose messaging. It was nothing but faded filters and silliness.

I TRIED AN OPEN-TO-ALL POLICY AT FIRST. THE INITIAL group was small, maybe only ten people, and a few of my girlfriends brought their boyfriends or husbands. We all knew one another. We were gender-inclusive and multiracial and came from a wide range of backgrounds. The first book we read was by Ta-Nehisi Coates, *Between the World and Me.*

There were a lot of things to love about that first meeting. The book itself, of course, which was visceral and important, a now-classic take on race and growing up Black in America. Like me, Coates had graduated from Howard University, and some of the other people in the club had gone to other HBCUs, as well, so we started the meeting with an instant connection. In no time at all, we were comparing notes and sharing personal anecdotes, and it got very emotional—deep in the best kind of way. As soon as it was over, I knew that I wanted to do it again.

But there were also aspects of that meeting that I wanted to change. When I thought about the conversation, I realized that I had been editing myself—being self-conscious in a way that I'm not normally—because there were so many men present. And those men were lovely men, people I liked very much, but they were doing the majority of the talking. They were dominating the conversation, and several times I found myself not saying what I wanted to say because I was worried about what they would think. I didn't want that. I didn't want to second-guess what came out of my mouth, or have to self-critique. As well-meaning as those men were, I didn't want me—or any other woman in the club—to have to struggle with the limitations the male presence brought into the room. I wanted to speak in an unfiltered, vulnerable, and honest way, and listen to other people do the same, and I knew that I would only find the comfort to do that with other women. Particularly Black women.

When I met Naomi Jackson in the Greenlight Bookstore, another aspect of the club became clear. She was a brand-new author; her debut novel, *The Star Side of Bird Hill,* was just starting to get all the critical attention it would eventually receive. Naomi was radiant and warm, with an infectious laugh. She was from Brooklyn, but her people were originally from Antigua, and her book, a beautiful coming-of-age story that tackled the pain and complications of growing up in a family that had been touched by mental illness, spoke to me in a personal way. I grabbed the opportunity. I showed her my Insta page, and I told her about my nascent book club. I warned her about how small and new it was, and then I invited her to attend as a visiting author. Lucky for me, she was gracious enough to accept my invitation.

Her excitement sparked something in me; I loved the enthusiasm she had about her work, and it occurred to me that many new authors would be equally passionate. I realized that debut writers had something special to offer and might be particularly interested in sharing with their readers. That maybe their fresh success would prime them to want to discuss the aspects of their craft and the parts of the process that they had only so recently mastered themselves.

That second club meeting was so much better than the first. Of course, the thrill of having a real live author there to discuss her work elevated things to a whole new level, but I also seemed to have hit upon a formula that really worked: a gathering of women, primarily Black women, reading a debut novel, also by a Black woman, in the kind of welcoming and safe space that allowed for true intimacy and exploration.

After that, we began to root and grow. Naomi introduced me to Angela Flournoy, who had just debuted with her book *The Turner House.* It was another story I could viscerally understand, about a large, multigenerational Detroit family and their struggle to keep the memories of their past ancestors alive in the face of drug abuse and generational trauma. About a week after she joined us at book club, Angela was nominated for a PEN America Literary Award and was also declared a National Book Award finalist. I once again felt the pleasure of "discovering" an author just before they hit it big. Of course, my ten-person book club and I didn't have anything to do with these authors' successes, but I couldn't help feeling like I was my own mini version of Oprah, illuminating beautiful work under my own, very small, spotlight.

It went on that way for about a year: Club meetings grew exponentially, I searched out new authors who were telling stories that addressed things that I was personally working through or felt curious about, and our Instagram page attracted more and more interest from the public. I started a monthly newsletter, which was basically, *Hello, everybody! This is what I'm reading! These are the new releases I'm excited about! This is what's happening this month in sisterhood!* And that became more and more popular as well. People were starting to respond. I got letters and emails from women thanking me for making the space and building the platform.

I never saw myself in literature before this, they wrote. *Thank you for holding up a mirror.*

A book club member wrote to me. We had a lot in common. She was also first generation whose parents had emigrated from Nigeria. Her family struggled with the same duality as mine: being Nigerian and wanting to hold on to that identity but living in the United States. We were close to the same age. She had moved to New York to pursue her creative dreams, and, like my family, her family had also been complicated by mental illness.

We ended up becoming close friends. We started emailing back and forth and she joined the book club. But even before we met in person, her email crystallized something for me. Well-Read Black Girl had grown into more. Something consequential. It was no longer just about my own little group of friends and the personal energy and good feelings that we gleaned from reading and talking. That energy had expanded to a point where they were somehow also consoling and empowering people in much bigger ways. Her vulnerability and gratitude made me realize that the club wasn't really about me anymore. Total strangers were finding it and using it and being inspired and encouraged and seen. We were filling a need. Well-Read Black Girl had become so much more than a social event or a book club. It started to feel like a call to action. When I started the book club, I was always searching for big questions. Curiosity was the precursor for every meeting. In the beginning, the authors that attended our meetups were debut writers. I was in complete awe of their achievement and made it known. I opened each session with standard book club fare, inquiring about their writing processes, plot devices, and characters. But once that was done, I wanted to know more about how they found their way in the world. What were their origin stories? What intrigued them? What stories did they return to again and again for comfort? What poems made them weep or laugh unexpectedly? What made them proclaim the title "writer"?

As a community, we shared our adoration for each author. Our book club became our sanctuary. My friend Misa called it "creative church." Each book surprised us with new revelations. A sentence that would transform your worldview, or a life-saving character that made you forgive yourself or someone who had broken your heart.

In my case, after reading *The Star Side of Bird Hill*, I found a way to forgive my mother. Noami Jackson's debut was extraordinary. In the story, you meet sixteen-year-old Dionne and ten-year-old Phaedra Braithwaite, who are forced to spend the summer in Barbados with their grandmother, while their mother, Avril, stays behind in Brooklyn to recover from a long depression. A depression.

This coming-of-age story felt familiar and honest. I had never read a story about young girls living with their mother's depression. I finally felt seen and my experience validated.

THE WRITERS THAT WE WELCOMED INTO OUR FOLD WERE undeniably talented. Naomi Jackson. Ibi Zoboi. Nic Stone. Kaitlyn Greenidge. Britt Bennett. Nicole Blades. Nicole Dennis-Benn. Renee Watson. Mahogany L. Browne. Jacqueline Woodson. Tia Williams. At book club, they had our undivided attention. I wanted them to feel loved by everyone in the room. We had read their masterpieces and found meaning on the pages. The authors had given us inspiration for deeper discussions and self-reflection. Together we discussed the intersections of Black womanhood—from womanist theory to reproductive rights to inequality in the workplace. At the heart of it, we were trying to find a way to collectively convey our thoughts and feelings. The book club answered a multitude of questions, forged new friendships, and made us interpret our own desires. There was a particular kind of hope we encountered with each title. *Maybe this will be the story that will transform my life, maybe even save it.*

IN 2016, I WAS INTERVIEWED ABOUT THE CLUB BY A RE-porter at *Brooklyn* magazine. Even now, reading the subtitle of that article gives me anxiety: *"Glory Edim Is the Future of Reading."*

When the article came out, everything suddenly exploded. The club had been steadily gaining popularity, but outside of our small community, no one had really known who I was. We would have our meetings, maybe I'd post a recap on Instagram after, and then I would pick the next book. But this article transformed our space—and my life. Suddenly publishers started to take heed and send me galleys. Literary agents reached out. Other magazines and newspapers called, wanting to write about the club. And we started to talk about doing something much bigger than the book club. We started to talk about doing a festival.

IN MAY 2017, I WAS INVITED TO A GALA ON THE UPPER WEST Side to honor Toni Morrison and James Patterson. I was incredibly nervous. This was one of the first times I had been extended a professional invitation to this kind of event, and I had no idea what to expect. But it was Toni Morrison. *Toni. Morrison.*

For a moment, I considered not going. I had never seen Toni Morrison in person, and there was a part of me that was terrified about the possibility of meeting her. Not because I thought she would disappoint me in any way, but because I already felt so satisfied just being in her public presence. I knew she was aware of me to some degree because of the work I'd done and all the public declarations I had made about her. We also had a friend in common, an actor who had worked on some of her audiobooks, and he told me that they had chatted about me a time or two. But I was content just knowing her through her books. I felt like she had already offered me unimaginable gifts. I didn't know that I needed any more than that.

Also, I would be lying if I didn't say that I worried that she'd think everything I was doing—the club, my Instagram account—was frivolous. How dare I talk to Toni Morrison, a literary hero, about my little posts on social media?

But I shook it all off. Of course I was going to go. It was Toni Morrison.

I KNEW THAT GETTING FROM GREENPOINT, BROOKLYN (where I was working at Kickstarter) to the Upper West Side would take the better part of an hour, so I wouldn't have time to go back home to change after work. I wasn't sure what people wore to these sorts of events, so I picked out a workhorse of a little black dress that I figured I could convert from day to night with a few well-chosen accessories. I remember sitting on the subway on the way uptown, trying to shut out everyone around me as I carefully redid my lipstick on the swaying train.

The moment I got there I knew I had woefully underestimated the dress code. It was in the ballroom at the Essex House, and the event was black tie. Men were in tuxedos, and women were in full-length ballgowns. My little black dress was not even close to appropriate. I may as well have showed up in yoga pants and a tank top.

Horrified, I hesitated at the threshold of the room, noting that the crème of the publishing world was in attendance, and wondering whether I should just turn my underdressed self right back around and go buy a slice instead.

Toni Morrison, I reminded myself. *Toni. Morrison.* And that was enough to propel me into the room.

After that it wasn't so bad. No one cared about my dress. I'd missed lunch that day, and there was champagne and endless platters of hors d'oeuvres being circulated around the room. I spent the first twenty minutes calculating how many tiny salmon tarts and cucumber rolls I could put away without anyone noticing.

The crowd was not only very well dressed but also very white, so it was a relief when I spotted another Black woman with a gorgeous hairstyle standing over by the bar. I recognized her immediately. Tayari Jones had yet to write her incredibly successful novel *An American Marriage,* but I had read and loved *Silver Sparrow,* and I felt a little thrill when she met my eyes and smiled.

We ended up spending the rest of the evening together, talking about her work and my book club. Tayari was enthusiastic and funny and incredibly encouraging about Well-Read Black Girl, asking me all sorts of questions about how it might grow next.

At the end of the evening, we were finally introduced to

Toni Morrison. Someone offered to take our picture, and I felt like I was floating with joy as Tayari and I flanked her on either side, the only three Black women in the room.

After the party, Tayari, who also lived in Brooklyn, offered to share a cab back home. On the hour-long drive, we continued to talk about Well-Read Black Girl, and I told Tayari that I was hoping to organize a literary festival at some point in the future.

"Why wait?" she answered. "Do it this year! People are excited about you now! Raise the money, and I'll be your keynote speaker!" Now, Tayari Jones is a very beautiful woman. Her smile, warm and genuine, lights up her face. She radiates an inner grace that naturally inspires. I sat in the car, slightly stunned by her generosity. Her sudden belief in me made everything feel possible. It was the first magical step in our friendship.

In the moment, it felt like serendipity and pure luck, but when I thought about it later, I realized it was yet another example of a Black woman I had just met responding to both me and the club with the most amazing generosity and enthusiasm. It was my community once again stepping up and helping me build something great. Five months later, on September 9, Tayari Jones was, indeed, our keynote speaker. We had raised $30,000 on Kickstarter, and more than eight hundred people attended the festival to share their love of reading the words of Black women.

Watching Tayari address the audience gave me chills. She spoke about the origin of our community. She told the story of our first meeting with Toni Morrison, how I had asked, and how she'd said yes in return. "You're currently in a room surrounded by other Black women who really want to help you," she said to the audience. "They want to say *yes* to you. So turn to your neighbor and do so!"

Author Naomi Jackson told this beautiful story about Lorraine Hansberry, and how when she wrote, she looked back on Lorraine and all her literary ancestors and the people who inspired her. She talked about the fact that we were all constantly looking both backward and forward, how there was an infinite line of connections that tie us all together.

As I looked around, I felt that. I viscerally sensed that connection, those ties. The women who came before us, the women who were there in the room, and the women who would come after us, united by our love of words and stories, community and truth.

CHAPTER TWELVE

Sonia Sanchez, "A Poem for My Father," "Just Don't Ever
Give Up on Love"

Sometimes just a title is enough to catch me by surprise. Take me by the throat. Send me someplace I've been trying to pretend doesn't actually exist.

It was a bright and cold winter day. I was wrapped in a blanket, a cup of tea by my side, reading a book of poetry by Sonia Sanchez in my living room. Sanchez, the embodiment of the Black Arts movement, has a gift for channeling everyday individuals, living and dead, and displaying their decency and humanity. She holds conversations with her characters in her poems. I sipped my tea and enjoyed my happy bubble, that state of literary absorption that can feel like a world of its own.

And then I turned the page.

"A Poem for My Father."

I put the book down and closed my eyes. Fixated. Thinking. Feeling much too much.

There are probably dozens, hundreds, maybe thousands of poems with this same title. Most people have things they want to say to their fathers. But on that day, that moment, reading that book, this particularly simple title shook me so hard that I swear I could hear my own teeth rattle.

If I could write like Sonia Sanchez, if I could channel her ability to speak to the dead, to have conversations with her ancestors, to call out to those who no longer walk on this earth, what words would I choose for my father? What poem would I write?

Perhaps I would just repeat the most important things I've ever said to him. "I love you / I miss you / I'm so proud to be your daughter."

Maybe I would make a Morrison-like list of all the things I didn't get to say: "You were enough / I love you despite the things that you did or didn't give us / Even when you disappointed me / I could always see that you were trying."

Maybe the poem would just be this:

I
Thought
We
Had
More
Time.

IT WAS LATE AUGUST 2017. MY BROTHER MAURICE WAS VIS-iting me in New York City with his girlfriend, Karimah. I lived in Brooklyn, but we were in Manhattan, in the Village, walking with my best friend, Ida, and her boyfriend, Kenny. It was after midnight, the air warm and balmy but no longer stifling. Summer was starting to fade away. We had just left a party, so we were a little buzzed, a little tired, but not ready to end our night. My brother lived in D.C. and didn't get up to the city that often, so I was determined to show him a New York time.

We were laughing and teasing each other. Joking around. I was the kind of happy I only ever felt when I had Maurice nearby.

My phone rang, and I didn't recognize the number, but I could see from the code that someone was calling me from Nigeria. That was strange because there was a six-hour time difference. It was very early in the morning back home.

I didn't think it was my father—he never called at this time. He was not an early riser, nor would he ever risk waking me up by calling me so late. I thought maybe it was another family member, one who hadn't made the time difference calculations.

"Hello?" I said, smiling at Maurice as he clowned around with his girlfriend, doing a little dance step on the street.

It was my father's wife.

"Glory? Your father wants to talk to you."

I was surprised but pleased. What a fun coincidence that Dad called when Maurice and I were together for the first time in months. I waved my brother over.

"Hi, Daddy! I'm actually with Maurice! Let me put you on speaker! What's going on!"

"Oh, my princess, I just called to say hello. I wanted to say that I love you guys. I was just thinking of you."

There's a thing about Nigerian culture. No one wants to deliver bad news. If something serious is happening, you are expected to be able to read between the lines and then continue to make casual chitchat. No one ever says, "Hey, I'm really sick" or "Listen, there is something I have to tell you." They just call you at an odd hour, tell you they love you, and leave you to figure out the rest.

But standing in a street in Manhattan, I didn't remember this polite societal Nigerian quirk. I just knew that Maurice and I were in the middle of having a good time with our friends and that our phone connection was fuzzy.

"Daddy?" I shouted. "Daddy? We're outside, and we can barely hear you. Can I call you back tomorrow morning?"

"Sure, sure," he said. His voice was faint, distant. "I love you guys."

"We love you! We love you! We'll call you in the morning!"

I didn't understand. I thought I would call him back in the morning. We were out on the town, ready to find another adventure, and the reception wasn't clear. I thought my dad was just missing me a little bit, so he had called to say hello.

Twenty minutes later, we were still walking, eating folded-up slices of pizza, arguing about whether we should go back to Brooklyn, and suddenly I thought of my father and that phone call, and I got a bad feeling.

I didn't want to worry Maurice, so I hung back a bit, letting him get ahead of me, and I called my mom. "Hey,

Mommy. I got a weird call from Daddy a little bit ago. We're outside and I'm not sure what's going on, but can you try to get through?"

"Sure, sure," said my mother. Of course, she understood Nigerian social niceties. They were in her bones. She must have known immediately. But she didn't say anything to worry me.

She called me back a few moments later, continuing the charade. "I couldn't get through. I'm sure he's fine. Just busy. I'll call again in the morning."

And by the morning, he was gone.

MY FATHER WAS A CHILD SOLDIER IN THE BIAFRAN WAR. His father had been one of the original Biafran secessionists and was murdered for his involvement early on in the conflict. At thirteen, my father was separated from the remainder of his family and enlisted to fight for the rebellion against the Nigerian government.

Even if you don't know much about the Biafran War, you have probably seen the searing images of small African children with sticks for arms and legs and a balloon for a belly that were shown around the world. Those children, that genocide-by-starvation of the Igbo and other minority groups (including ours, the Efiks), was a product of the Biafran War. The blockade created by the Nigerian army against the secessionists killed over half a million people. Thousands of people died of starvation each day.

I didn't think much about this as a child. Our family was

living in the United States by then. And the idea of my father being a child soldier (or that there was even such a thing at all) never crossed my mind. My father never talked to me about his time in the army. (Nor does my mother ever talk to me about her experience. Though I do know that she, too, was separated from her family for over a year when she was twelve, and that she also lost family members to the war.) All I knew was that he had fought on the losing side of a war, and despite that, still wished for an independent state from Nigeria. Even if he didn't tell war stories, he made it clear that he believed in the ideals he had gone to battle for at so tender an age.

It wasn't until after he died that I learned the details of his experience. I learned that any sense of stability he grew up with—his education, his home and religious life, his daily interactions—were all permanently interrupted by the war. It was only after he died that I realized that the experience of living through something like that—war, famine, being separated from your family, being conscripted into an army as a child, being forced to surrender to the same army who mercilessly starved the people you loved—must have caused immense trauma to my father's psyche. It was only after he died that I was able to piece together certain things that I had never quite understood about my father.

And maybe it was only after he died, and I was given this information about his past, that I fully forgave him for leaving me behind.

———

WHEN MY MOTHER CALLED ME THE NEXT MORNING TO tell me that my dad had passed away, I was in shock. I knew that my father was ill, but I had no idea that he was dying. He had been diagnosed with cancer (just what kind he'd always been politely and insistently vague about) two years earlier. I had panicked at first, trying to find different hospitals or cancer treatments in the United States that might accept him as a patient. But I didn't have much money or influence, I was still living with roommates, and my father refused to give me any details of his illness. I would call the treatment centers, and they would ask for blood tests and details on his state of health. I would feel so foolish and helpless, not knowing the most basic things about his situation, but still desperate to find a way to help him.

When I talked to him and complained about this, he chided me and told me to stop worrying. I didn't need to take care of him. He had traveled to Dubai and London for care. He was getting better. He was in remission. The treatments he'd had overseas had worked.

I wanted to go to Nigeria so I could see this for myself. It had been four years since I'd last seen him in person, and though he looked and sounded strong enough over phone calls and Skype sessions, I knew that communicating that way could never show the real truth of a situation. I knew I wouldn't feel better until I could hug him and gauge his health up close. But my mother discouraged me. She pointed out that I didn't have the money. That I needed a visa. That if my dad wasn't feeling well, he wouldn't be able to pick me up from the airport. "Wait until he's better," she advised.

What she didn't tell me was that she'd had a dream, a premonition, that he would die soon. And she knew that, no matter what, I would have to return to Nigeria to bury my father, and I would not be able to afford two trips. So she chose the dead over the living. My filial duty over my chance to see my father that one last time.

My dad wasn't lying, though. He was getting better. He was stronger. His cancer was in remission. But his immune system was weak from the treatments, and then he caught pneumonia, and after that it was only a matter of days.

SONIA SANCHEZ WROTE A SHORT STORY, OR MAYBE IT WAS a true story, called "Don't You Ever Give Up on Love." It revolves around something that happened to her while she was sitting in the park and writing. The narrator encounters this older, wiser woman, who tells the narrator a bit of her own life story and ends up giving the narrator a new perspective on life. The older woman says that she doesn't ever look at the harder parts of her life as failures or mistakes because they were just part of her life and her continuum. She basically says, "I experienced all these things, I had some hardships, but I never gave up on love."

After he left me, after my father went back to Nigeria, I thought he had given up on love. Or at least, that he had given up on loving me. And even after we were reunited a decade later, I still questioned why he had left.

My father kept secrets. He had multiple lives and he was driven by a need to obtain influence. He sometimes drank to excess. He wished for reverence and a legacy that could not be erased. He wanted to put his memory into the bricks of a building. He wanted to run for office. He wanted his name to be known and remembered.

These things used to torture me. I loved him so much, and I couldn't understand why our small, happy life—our family—in America hadn't been enough for him. I couldn't understand what force could have possibly driven him from my side.

But I think any survivor of war must live with a constant yearning for a new beginning. I think they must always be in two places at once, the present and the past. I think they long for things that they can call their own, even as they are so painfully aware of how quickly things can be taken away. I think when you see true obliteration—of a person, a building, an entire society—it must make you wonder what is real, what can possibly survive. I believe that my father must have been afraid of that very thing, of disappearing. I think that he saw so many lives that ended before they even really began, so many corpses, so many children who never grew up, and maybe that was what moved him to push so desperately against being forgotten.

So much so that it took him away from me, even if he never gave up on our love.

MY MOTHER, BROTHER, AND I LEFT FOR NIGERIA A FEW days after his death. It was my first time traveling back home with Maurice, and it felt bittersweet. I had been to Nigeria twice as an adult, but my brother hadn't been home since he was twelve. Now we were in our thirties, but we were still like children, pointing out the window as we drove through our village. "Did you see this? Did you see that?" It was lovely to see the town through my brother's eyes. To have someone to share the trip with. But we both wished Maurice had come back sooner. We both hated the fact that our father would not be there to greet us at his house, to smile and laugh and take us to the bar so he could show off his American children to the other villagers.

Grief makes time slow down. Every moment of that visit seemed to stretch and bend. There was, of course, nothing easy about burying our father, but things were made even worse by the bad blood between us and my father's wife. She had done her best to deny us any inheritance—even being so petty as to refuse to give Maurice my father's college ring from Howard—but my father had secretly gone to a separate lawyer and drawn up a will that bequeathed his house to me and Maurice. My stepmother and her daughters would be able to stay there until she either remarried or died, but after that the house would become ours. It didn't help that my mother was there with us as well. In Nigeria, the first marriage, even after a divorce, was always considered the real thing. My mother was still seen as my father's true wife. My stepmother was bitter and angry at what she felt was a betrayal of the highest order—to the point where she refused to let us stay in our father's house, and we had to couch hop among various relatives instead.

We hardly slept. Because we were Americans, Maurice

was certain we'd be robbed, waking every fifteen minutes to jump up and look out the window. His paranoia made me paranoid, too. The two of us woke up each morning exhausted by our ridiculous fear.

My dad was a traditionalist in many ways, but he had always given me my autonomy. He didn't care that I was female. He believed in me, made me feel like I could do anything. And he had shielded me from certain cultural realities whenever I'd visited him before. But now, without my father there to insist I be included in the conversation, people would approach me and Maurice and turn away from me to ask how Maurice was doing: How did he feel, what did he think? They would ask him if he was going to come back home and take my father's place, start a business. "I can get you a job!" they'd insist.

And I'd stand there, waiting for them to acknowledge me. The older child. The one who had found her father, had come back to see him, who loved him so much. And there would be nothing. All eyes on Maurice. All concern for his father's son.

This situation did allow me to learn things about my dad I had never known before. People were eager to talk to Maurice about our father. To tell him things they would never have bothered to tell me. "Eh, your father, your father," they'd say, "let me tell you about your father." And I would be allowed to stand there and quietly listen.

This is when I started to learn about my father's time in the war.

———

AT THE FUNERAL I WORE A WIG BECAUSE I HAD LET MY hair go natural and that was unacceptable in Nigeria. Women's hair had to be straight or permed, or you were considered unkempt. I was too tired to straighten my hair and too fragile to bear the criticism, hence the wig. And in the church, I wore a headwrap over the wig. But apparently that was not proper, either. I was scolded because my hair was not as fully covered as it should have been.

I had written something about my father that I wanted to read, but I was firmly told that it would not be possible: A daughter does not speak at her father's funeral. A woman does not speak in church. I was told not to worry; Maurice could speak for us both.

No, I thought. *No, I have things I need to say.*

When Maurice got up, I got up, too. We walked to the pulpit together, and I could hear the gasps of horror, the tongue sucking, the tsks of disapproval, as people watched us pass by. But nobody moved to stop me. They must have decided that it wasn't worth trying to teach this rude American woman the way things should be done.

My brother and I spoke together, moving between English and Efik. I knew that people were unimpressed by my accent (Maurice's was better) and offended that I was up there at all, but I continued to speak. I needed to honor my dad.

After the funeral, I sat with my mother, and she told me about a dream she'd had the night before, how my father had come to her, comforted her, talked to her. And I was so angry. Why hadn't he come to me? Where was my dream?

———

PEOPLE USED TO SAY THAT I WAS JUST LIKE MY FATHER IN SO many ways. They said that we had the same sense of tenacity, the same audacity, that we both persevered. I liked to think that when hard things happened, we both tried to be courageous, to lean into the storm. Friends said that we were both warm, open, trusting. Sometimes to a fault. Like me, my father always seemed to see the good in people. He walked into every situation insisting that things would work out, that people almost always had the best of intentions.

Now I wonder how he could have lived through what he did, seen what he saw, and still trust in the basic decency of human beings. My mother is the opposite. She assumes everyone is lying. She expects betrayal. She trusts no one. Considering all she went through, her outlook makes much more sense to me.

Sometimes I think that maybe my father was not as sunny and carefree as he seemed. Maybe my father drank and lied and cheated and left because he carried things that most of us cannot begin to comprehend. What happens to you when you're on the losing end of a genocide? What happens when you watch hundreds of thousands of children slowly die, and the people who killed them are allowed to win? Who do you become when you watch the people you love systematically become erased from this earth? When first their bodies, then their souls, and then their names fade away, forgotten?

My father left me and my brother a house, and that was an enormous gift. Home is everything to me. Having a family home in Nigeria allows us to keep connections and ties that I thought we had lost for good. I used to think that my father stopped loving me when he left, but I know now that this inheritance was meant to prove that he didn't. He worked so hard for this house. He designed and built it himself. And he was thinking of us the entire time. But now, I also think that maybe another, more painful gift he tried to leave us was his own protective silence. He didn't tell me about his past. He didn't share what he knew about the dark side of humanity. He never let on that sometimes, evil wins. He carried this pain and this horror inside himself and only showed me his sweetness, his humor, his faith, his love. Maybe he left us not only to build us a house—to find respectability and success and worldly things—but also to keep his secrets and his silence. To distance us from these demons that he surely carried and battled within himself every day.

THEY NAMED A STREET FOR MY FATHER. IT RUNS PAST OUR house and curls up around the little cemetery on our land, where my father lies buried. I like to think about how pleased he would have been had he known that his name would carry on in such a public way. But I always carry the compulsion to honor him with something more. A street isn't enough. My father wanted to be remembered in the grandest of styles. I am constantly thinking about how to fulfill that desire.

I talk to him sometimes. I reassure him. *Daddy, I remember you. And I'm so proud to be your daughter. And I will continue to live my life to honor who you were and what you taught me. My son will know your name through me, and someday he will tell his child your name. You will not be forgotten.*

I wish I could give him a poem. Unfortunately, poetry is not my strength. I am not uncomfortable with words, but I am not Sonia Sanchez, either.

So I offer him—and my mother and my brothers and my son—something else; not a poem but a love letter.

These words, this chapter, this book. I write our names, I tell our stories, I use my words to light our truth. I tell the hard things and the beautiful things. I force myself to remember. I don't allow myself to look away. I never give up on our love. I stay.

Unlike my father, unlike my mother, I break our silence. I choose to lean into our family storm.

CHAPTER THIRTEEN

Toni Morrison, *Beloved*

So you protected yourself and loved small. Picked the tiniest stars out of the sky to own; lay down with head twisted in order to see the loved one over the rim of the trench before you slept. Stole shy glances at her between the trees at chain-up. Grassblade, salamanders, spiders, woodpeckers, beetles, a kingdom of ants. Anything bigger wouldn't do. A woman, a child, a brother—a big love like that would split you wide open in Alfred, Georgia. He knew exactly what she meant: to get to a place where you could love anything you chose—not need permission for desire—well now, that was freedom.

The next time I fall in love, I am going to pick the biggest star. I am going to dream the biggest thing I can imagine, and then say it out loud. I am going to choose the person who sees me the clearest. I am going to find someone who has an overflowing abundance of tenderness to share. I am going to find a man who is full of words.

When I started dating seriously at Howard, I prided myself on not having a "type." I was drawn to ambitious energy and creativity. I didn't have a list of must-have characteristics and dealbreakers for boyfriends. There was no mandatory height requirement or the need to make X amount of money. I simply wanted a partner who would make me laugh and support my dreams. This led to me dating without reservation: men who were aspiring emergency room doctors, first-year law students, stand-up comedians, and a lot of African American studies majors.

Kojo was a creative. When we first met, I found him painfully awkward yet inventive. He had a kind smile that held a wide gap that you couldn't miss. We were both enamored with art and with looking for ourselves: in books, in documentaries, anywhere we could find reflections of ourselves. We had one significant thing in common: growing up as a first-generation American. That is, being the American-born child of African immigrants. Together we embodied a mash-up of the cultures and aspirations of Howard's campus. His pursuit was slow and steady. Our friendship grew. Kojo loved documentary films and hip-hop music. His obsessions with Nelson George and Pharrell Williams was unmatched. Early in our relationship, we lingered in art galleries in Chelsea and had nonsensical debates about the state of Black politics. We met at Howard in undergrad but didn't date seriously until we both lived in New York. After our first date, I knew immediately that I loved his grin. We exchanged emails that simply read: *I miss you* or *I love you.* He coined my favorite nickname, "Puff," because of my signature afro. Kojo introduced me to the sounds of Richie Havens and to experi-

mental films by Arthur Jafa. We discussed the sonic bril-
liance of Roy Ayers Ubiquity and the meditative teachings of
Paulo Coelho. I shared my admiration for Edwidge Danticat,
Lorna Simpson, and Lynn Nottage. We wandered around
the Strand bookstore for hours. We watched the premiere of
An Oversimplification of Her Beauty and traveled to Montreal
on a whim. He took me on a surprise date to see the play
Sweat, and got us front-row seats at Gregory Porter's annual
Valentine's Day concert. We spent many weekends in Hud-
son Valley, and once took a road trip to Montauk, where I
insisted on stealing the hotel towels. They weren't luxurious
towels but were instead rough and scratchy. Kojo was una-
mused by my theft. But whenever I used them, I would re-
call our absurd adventure to East Hampton; eating messy
lobster rolls and trying to catch the sunset. Over time, we fell
in love. I thought he possessed so many of the qualities I desired in a life partner. He was ambitious, funny, generous,
and patient. Most important, I thought he was full of potential.

HE AND I WERE LIVING IN A TINY FOURTH-FLOOR APART-
ment in Brooklyn. I hated that apartment. But the one good
thing was that we had access to the rooftop. He, especially,
was so enamored with that rooftop. He loved the sky. He
loved fireworks. And when we were up there, we could see
the Brooklyn Bridge, and we could see the lights of the city
all spread out in front of us. It felt like we were part of this
bigger thing. It felt like a place between heaven and earth.

But that night, we were fighting on the rooftop. We'd

been together on and off for eight years, after moving to New York in 2012. On the roof, we were drinking wine and, okay, maybe not fighting exactly but dragging out a fight that we'd had earlier in the day. I was doing what I always did. I was asking for more communication. I was suggesting therapy. I was trying to express what I needed to change. I was telling him that I worried about our connection. I was pressing him to talk to me, to show that he heard me, to move forward, to evolve.

And he was doing what he always did. He was watching the sky, the bridge. He was defending himself. He was drinking his wine and probably only half listening to me, and sometimes saying things that he thought I wanted to hear.

And then it was late and I was tired, so I decided that I had said the things I needed to say and that he was probably not going to say the things I wanted to hear, and so we should go back downstairs and go to bed.

I walked down ahead of him and stepped into the kitchen, and then I turned around, and he was on one knee, holding up a ring box, and smiling at me.

I don't remember what he said. It might have been as simple as, "Will you marry me, Glory?" I just remember feeling flustered. And emotionally depleted from our rooftop conversation. And confused, because how could he think that this was the right time or the right place?

I tried to move past him, to step back out of our cluttered kitchen.

He stood up. He blocked my way, still smiling. Still holding out the box.

"Did you talk to my mother?" I asked.

And he frowned. Annoyed, I think, that I would bring my mother into this moment. But if he knew me at all, he would have known that when I got engaged, I would want my family involved. That I would never want a moment this important to go without their presence to share in the joy.

Or maybe he *did* know me that well. Maybe he did know that was what I would want. But it wasn't what *he* wanted.

"Is that a yes?" he answered.

I hesitated—a split second—and he just sort of shut down. His face went blank. He pulled the ring box away.

I felt terrible.

"I—I just need to think about it," I said. And then, trying to lighten the mood, "Can I see the ring?"

"No," he said and put the box back into his pocket. Stopped talking.

And I never saw that ring. Because he never bothered to ask me if I had thought through things, and I was afraid to tell him what I knew, deep down, to be true.

IN THE BEGINNING IT FELT LIKE THE ART AND ENERGY OF New York sustained us. Exploring the city with Kojo was an endless quest. He was the first person I wanted to share every new fascination with. I saved all of our theater playbills and ticket stubs in a memory box. One day we'd show our kids, I thought. Admittedly, we were young, clueless, and ambitious. We encouraged each other constantly, to apply for the job, make the film, write the book, travel the world, follow the passion to the very end at all costs. It was all in reach because we believed in each other. I loved our creative relationship more than I loved my own ambition. It felt good to cheer on someone that I believed so adamantly in. I wanted to be his wife and start a family. But it wasn't a perfect relationship. Nothing is. Despite our creative connections, there was a lingering mistrust. We struggled to be reliable with each other. When we would argue, Kojo would emotionally disappear, and I'd feel abandoned. We'd break up and get back together. We'd keep circling around the same problems repeatedly. Lying by omission. Avoiding conflict. Pretending things were okay when they were not. Our creative connections couldn't make up for what we lacked in emotional maturity and honest communication. I kept wanting his smile to solve everything, but it wasn't enough. Despite all the clear signs, I stayed with Kojo, hoping that we could write a new story.

AND THEN WE WERE LIVING IN LOS ANGELES, IN A BIG IN-dustrial loft that we had rented from his friend. I was pregnant. The loft was in Downtown L.A., and it felt so cold, the floor and ceiling made of gray concrete. There was no place for a nursery.

I was dreaming of what our baby's room would look like, with a star and moon theme, a certain color for the walls, a particular rocking chair where I could sit and nurse our child. Instead, we put a crib and a borrowed bureau into the spare room and waited for our due date.

We had come to L.A. to be closer to his family. His father

was diagnosed with cancer, and he wanted to be near his parents in case they needed him. I understood this. Of course I did. I knew how important it was to be there to help when your parents needed you.

Before we moved, he had talked about his parents all the time. He held up their forty-year marriage as an ideal, a blueprint. And I believed him, because what model did I have to point to? Who was I to say what marriage was supposed to look like?

But being in L.A. meant that I finally got to witness this storied relationship up close and personal, and it was not what he described. It was not what I had imagined.

There was a couch in his parents' house. It had been there since my partner was seven years old. He is now in his forties. It was stained and sagging, and his mother disliked it. She told me so.

I liked his mother. I felt protective of her. I worried because her light seemed so dim. Her husband was the one who was ill, but it was her light that was shrouded by these constant jabs he made at her expense. "Oh, come on, it's just a joke!" he would declare, after an unpleasant comment. And she would smile, always a good sport, but I could see the web of tension in the lines of her mouth. I could see the way her hands fell helpless at her sides. She seemed to be the one who truly needed care.

So I asked her why she couldn't buy a new couch.

She slowly shook her head. "Oh, no, no," she murmured. "I could never. He wouldn't allow it. He loves that couch. I can't replace that couch."

And I thought, *Is this normal? Maybe this is what marriage is supposed to look like? Maybe one person's soul necessarily dims in the harsher light of the other?*

Because what did I know? What did I know?

MY MOTHER LANDED IN LOS ANGELES A WEEK BEFORE MY due date. It was March 2020, just weeks into the Covid pandemic, and we were impatient for my son's arrival. In that in-between time, we walked cautiously around downtown Los Angeles wearing oversized sunglasses and N95 masks. We bounced between Whole Foods and a café where I obsessively ordered Boba tea. She accompanied me to doctor's appointments and told me stories of my childhood, fondly recalling when she'd given birth to me and my brothers. I was immensely grateful for her presence. She was warm and familiar.

AFTER GIVING BIRTH TO OUR SON, ZIKOMO, MY BODY WAS always confused, both bewildered and betrayed by all that my son needed. From the breastfeeding to the diaper changes, it all felt like too much. Each day, with his tiny head nestled in my chest, his hunger overwhelmed me. But I was also in awe. Kojo and I had made this perfect little person and our entire worlds had changed. It was as if giving birth had opened a chasm and it was impossible to seal it back up. Here was this infant that I loved more than anything and who constantly depleted me. Despite this, I was determined to push my body past its limits. I wanted to be his protector. I also become painfully aware that something between me and Kojo was amiss and the birth of our son wouldn't fix it. During our eight years together, we broke up and got back together numerous times. We moved in and out of Brooklyn apartments. There were new jobs, new arguments, and unspoken jealousies. We fought. We made up. And then we got pregnant.

I STRUGGLED TO DO EVERYTHING: TO SWADDLE, TO PUMP enough milk, to find my own gentle rhythm in motherhood. Every time I tried breastfeeding, my son would vigorously throw his head back in protest. I downloaded an app and manically tracked every feeding and diaper change. I purchased sound machines and complicated onesies that promised to ease his nighttime routine. But it was hopeless, he only slept when being held. When I tried to place Zikomo in the bassinet, he wailed and wailed. I felt a wave of instant guilt and strapped him to my chest. I would only let him go once my arms grew tried. Occasionally, his warm, sleepy body was passed to others throughout the day: from my mother to his father, and then back to my arms. We became an unexpected trio because of the pandemic. My mother made us meals and Kojo asked her question after question about Nigeria and what it was like when she first arrived in America. The banter was initially warm and inquisitive. Outside of our apartment loomed the recent murder of George Floyd and streets crowded with protesters. It was impossible to ignore the political unrest and collective agitation. Becoming a mother at the height of the pandemic was excruciating. Paired with my exhaustion and postpartum anxiety, whenever I stepped out of the house, I was full of anticipation. I was constantly looking for danger, whether it was airborne germs or erratic people on the street. After a few months, I realized I didn't like the vastness of California. I found everything too far and uninviting. Even the freeways left me terrified. All my life I had considered myself adventurous but now I wasn't sure. I was scared, and the reality of motherhood felt heavy, like a lifetime of responsibility and unbearable love. I finally understood my mother's fears. The unconditional love and constant fear happened all at once. Being a mother made me feel crazed and out of control. My own mother suddenly felt like an anchor. I was so grateful to share Zikomo with her, watching as she doted on him; gathering him up into her arms as he fussed, expertly fitting his floppy little head into the warm hollow between her shoulder and breast. He raised a hand to his mouth, sucked his finger, eyes half closed. She rubbed his back, stroked his hair, murmured in a voice too soft for me to make out her words. His little whimpers trailed off, his eyes drifted shut, and his breath became slow and steady. The sweet way she talked to him, the affection of her gaze as he slept in her arms, her tender and perpetual attention to his needs made me catch my own breath. I felt a sharp wave of sensation that flowed between regret, pain, and a perfect, healing kind of grace.

And when she left to return to D.C., two months later, I wanted to cry out, to plead.

Don't go! Don't go! Don't leave us here alone!

———

TONI CADE BAMBARA WROTE, "WORDS CONJURE." AND I know that to be true. I know that to be true because when my mother stopped speaking, her life almost slipped away from her. I know that to be true because when I found my father's letters, I was restored. I know that to be true because literal words have changed my story in such a powerful way.

And I know that to be true because when my partner ran out of words—when he stopped talking to me—I was quietly and totally shattered.

HE SAT ACROSS FROM ME AT OUR KITCHEN TABLE. I HELD our baby and picked up a conversation we had been circling for weeks, months even. "But maybe we can hire some help? Someone to come in, just for a few hours a day, so I can do a little more work? Take a little time?"

He looked at me. His eyes were tired. Then he slowly turned his head and looked away. As if I hadn't spoken at all. As if I wasn't there.

My partner, the father of my child, the same man who had given me my Well-Read Black Girl T-shirt, stopped talking to me while we were living under the same roof.

He had known me for over a decade. He knew everything there was to know. About my history. About my mother. And he knew exactly what using this particular weapon against me would do. And yet, from that day forward, he closed his mouth and looked away. He brought silence into our home.

AFTER I GAVE BIRTH TO ZIKOMO, MY LONELINESS INTENSI-fied and my self-doubt was relentless. I couldn't understand his father's behavior. The silent treatment, the secrecy, the complete disregard for my feelings. We were struggling yet pretending to be okay. All of our mistrust and tension filled our apartment. The Covid pandemic made it even worse; our relationship was unraveling under the pressure of parenthood and expectations. I wanted to move back to Washington, D.C., to be close to my family. I expected him to be honest, to be vulnerable; instead, he lied about insignificant things and avoided my questions. He expected me to be quiet and follow his lead.

When we first met I was young, naïve, and eager to smile my way through anything. I desperately wanted to be loved. Part of me longed to be rescued. I saw so much potential in our courtship. He was a "good guy." We'd have two kids, a dog, and a picket fence. Now I couldn't even fake smile. Instead, eight years later, we had an unintended pregnancy, and all the possibilities of our relationship felt unrealized. I felt foolish and ashamed by my predicament. The intimacy was gone, our conversations had become about the day-to-day logistics of caring for our son rather than anything more meaningful. The façade of it all left me exhausted; especially whenever he decided to withdraw into silence. After dealing with my mother's years of silence, my brain was hardwired to see his behavior as a rejection. Motherhood made every-thing feel raw, and his emotional distance triggered some-thing vast and unmeasurable.

Oddly, he didn't even notice my distress. Or maybe he simply ignored it. He certainly didn't respond to me in a lov-ing manner. My grief was heavy. Our rift just grew and grew. Over time, I felt emotionally unsafe in our relationship. It dawned on me that he cared more about how everything ap-peared than my actual feelings. He wanted to look good on-line, in front of his family; my feelings were secondary. I gazed into my son's eyes, wondering how could I possibly raise him while feeling unloved and ignored. As I sunk deeper into my depression, I instinctively picked up *all about love* by bell hooks. She writes:

> The essence of true love is mutual recognition—two individ-uals seeing each other as they really are. We all know that the usual approach is to meet someone we like and put our best self forward, or even at times a false self, one we believe will be more appealing to the person we want to attract. When our real self appears in its entirety, when the good behavior becomes too much to maintain or the masks are taken away, disappointment comes. All too often individuals feel, after the fact—when feelings are hurt and hearts are broken—that it was a case of mistaken iden-tity, that the loved one is a stranger. They saw what they wanted to see rather than what was really there.

Her words captured our dilemma. I was finally seeing our relationship for what it really was: fragile and lacking our truest selves. We both wanted to see what we wanted to see instead of the truth. I wanted a partner to save me, and he wanted to pretend that we were okay.

THE ONE THING I LIKED ABOUT THAT LOFT IN L.A. WAS THE courtyard in the center of the building. I would sometimes carry our son out into the courtyard, and we would sit there together and watch our neighbors pass through.

It took all my willpower to not grab every person who walked by and ask, *Is it normal for your partner to decide that he will only communicate with you through email, even if you're in the next room?*

Sometimes I would take the baby to the store, and we would stand in line at the checkout, and I would force myself not to turn around and say, *Is it normal for someone to simply refuse to answer even when you are begging him to speak to you?*

Before my son was born, I imagined how we'd raise him. I daydreamed about the type of person he might be. Would he be good at playing soccer? Would he read the *Narrative of the Life of Frederick Douglass*? Would he love Afro-beat and the sounds of Fela Kuti? He would surely have a warm smile like both of his parents. Now I would sit in the loft's floor-to-ceiling window and nurse my baby, and I would think, *Maybe it's normal for someone to know the one thing that would hurt you the most and then to use it to get what he wants. Maybe that's partnership. Maybe that's love.*

————

AT HOWARD, I HAD LEARNED THAT WHEN YOU ARE WORK-ing for the greater good, a bigger cause, it allows for a personal liberation as well. As the months passed, and my son grew older, he became my greater good, my bigger cause. He became the agent of my liberation.

I would watch him play on the floor, and I would think, *I don't want to raise him in a concrete home.*

I would kiss his sweet little forehead and think, *I don't want you to grow up seeing your parents give each other the silent treatment.*

I would nurse him as we sat in the living room together and think, *I don't want to face a forty-year-old couch.*

My baby wasn't talking yet, but sometimes I would take his cheeks in my hands, the same way I used to do with my little brothers, and I would pretend he was talking to me, providing both sides of our conversation.

And then later, I would realize it was the only time I'd spoken with anyone in days.

I refuse, I absolutely refuse, to let my son live in a family where silence is used as a weapon.

I'd heard of mothers described as their child's first home. I envisioned my physical body as a sturdy house. I was required to nurture, protect, and help my son grow strong from now until forever. If done correctly, our attachment would lead to a good start in life. That's all I wanted for Zikomo—a warm, bright home to grow into his best self. Yet I felt like I was unprepared. Absolutely nothing was like I expected it to be. And so, I gathered my son into my arms and left the silence behind. In the days leading up to our departure, I was always hearing my future voice in my head, "*if only you had left him and started over.*" I was convinced that our relationship was beyond repair. We boarded our flight and I started to pray. I wanted to spare my future self and my son. Once we landed in Washington D.C., we were suddenly a family of two.

"LOVE IS OR IT AIN'T. THIN LOVE AIN'T LOVE AT ALL."

The next time I fall in love, words will fly between us like shooting stars. The next time I fall in love, I will lay in my man's arms as he whispers all the things he loves about me, telling me the way he sees me. I will let his words roll over me, stoking my fire with his voice. The next time I fall in love, there will be endless poetry and prose and prayer between us. The next time I fall in love, we will sing together in the kitchen on rainy Sunday mornings. The next time I fall in love, we will yell when it is necessary; then we will sweeten our voices and make up, humming our forgiveness. The next time I fall in love, there will be jokes told, silliness and clowning, there will be laughter that rings through our whole home.

The next time I fall in love, our life will be filled with words.

CHAPTER FOURTEEN

Bill Martin, Jr., and Eric Carle, *Brown Bear, Brown Bear, What Do You See?*; Barack Obama, *A Promised Land*; Ta-Nehisi Coates, *Between the World and Me*; Roda Ahmed and Leandra Rose, *Good Night, Wiggly Toes*

Dear Zikomo,

Even before you were born, you had a huge library. Not just the library I have built up for myself over the years, which I hope you will also think of as yours someday, but a library of your very own. We have a lot of book friends, and when word went out that you were coming, the books just started pouring in. Everybody had a book to give you. Everyone had memories of a favorite book that their own child or grandchild had once demanded to be read over and over again. Everyone wanted to give you a book they had adored when they were a kid, a book they couldn't put down, a book that had changed their life. People love to give books, and they seemed to especially love giving books to you.

Brown Bear, Brown Bear, What Do You See? by Bill Martin, Jr., and Eric Carle was the first book I ever read to you.

You were so little that you couldn't hold your head up yet. Your eyes were still unfocused. The fontanelle in your skull hadn't closed. You sat propped into the crook of my arm, your fist almost entirely in your mouth, as I read the story and showed you the pictures, carefully holding up each page in front of your sweet little face. I showed you a brown bear, a red bird, a yellow duck, a blue horse, a green frog, a purple cat, a white dog, a black sheep, a goldfish, a teacher and some children. You drooled a little and kicked a little, your eyes got big, tracking the colors and shapes, and you seemed happy, content. I hoped then, as I hope now, that you would be a book person, too.

There are so many things I want for you, Zik, so many things I'm working toward making sure you have. Some material things: I want us to have a warm and safe family home. I want you to have an excellent education and a college fund. I want you to be able to travel and see the world and amass new experiences. And I have plans for making sure that those things come our way. But even if we don't end up having all—or even some—of those tangible things, if nothing else, we will always have these books and the lessons we have learned from them. That will be one of your most important inheritances from me.

YOUR MOMMY IS NOT A PERSON WHO DREAMS VERY MUCH.

Of course, I have a thousand hopes and plans for you, but I mean that I don't have many actual, literal dreams. Each night my head hits the pillow, and each morning I wake up, and I never seem to remember anything that happened in between.

This bothered me terribly just after your grandfather passed. I missed him so much and wanted to see him so badly. I closed my eyes each night hoping he would come to me, that he would find a spectral doorway that he could step through. But night after night, I was disappointed. My sleep remained as undisturbed as always.

But when I was pregnant with you, I think you gave me your dreams. Or maybe we were creating our dreams together. In any case, my nights were suddenly Technicolor. Because every time I closed my eyes, I was seeing your face and having long, wonderful conversations with you, or swimming with you in the vast, blue ocean, or flying through the stars with you in my arms. Or once, I was hovering above, looking down at an almost grown-up version of you as you stood in the yard at Howard University. (Listen, I want you to go to whatever college you choose. But get used to it, Zik—your mommy will talk about Howard a whole lot as you grow up.)

I must admit that I wasn't having the easiest time before you came along. I was feeling a little lost and shaken, not sure of my faith or my path. I had some big questions that I didn't know if I would ever receive answers to. And right after I realized that I was pregnant with you, the world was turned upside down by the Covid pandemic.

We all necessarily turned inward during lockdown, and for so many people, it was a scary and isolating time. But turning inward toward you brought me joy. How could I feel alone when you were growing inside of me day after day? How could I be bored when I had you to wonder about and ponder upon? Your light was so bright even before you were born. Carrying you in my womb, feeling you kick and somersault, knowing that there were two heartbeats syncopated inside my body, and having these vivid, wonderful dreams gave my world a center that I'd never had before. You opened up so many possibilities for me. I suddenly felt I was touching something bigger than myself, something greater even than the power of literature, or my attachment to my mother or brothers. You gave me a reason and a purpose. You brought me back to God and the universe. You gave me a sense of grace.

You gave me all that, my baby—these priceless things— before you even took your first breath. And I will spend my lifetime trying to repay you for those gifts.

I THINK A LOT ABOUT THE BOOKS I HOPE YOU WILL READ someday. There are hundreds, thousands—maybe as many as there are stars in the sky. There is a book called *Between the World and Me* by a wonderful writer and good man, someone I hope you will know someday, Ta-Nehisi Coates. In it, he writes a letter to his son, who was a little Black boy just like you are now. I thought of Ta-Nehisi and his book when I decided I wanted to write you this letter.

One of the main things that Ta-Nehisi wrote about is something that I also understand, something that all Black parents in America know about to some degree. I have so much unconditional love and uplift for you, my son, such high hopes and expectations, but I also worry. I feel so much fear. For parents with Black children in America, especially Black boys, the love and the fear necessarily exist side by side.

I can keep you safe and shielded in our home. I can give you love and validation and support. I can tell you that you can be anything, do anything, and I will mean every word I say. But outside the walls of our house, there are low expectations, and there is violence and there is racism and there is an entire world set up to make you feel less than. And I wouldn't be a good mother if I didn't warn you about that and prepare you to face those ugly and unfair things. But I also want you to understand that while you need to protect yourself when you can, and sometimes you will have to be very careful, you cannot allow yourself to be defeated by those vile things, either.

There are ways to fight, Zikomo. There are ways to stand against the fear. Don't let anyone denigrate you. Persevere. Have faith in yourself. Pick the good. Have compassion for yourself and others. Be a truth teller. Have a strong work ethic but an even stronger love ethic as well. Read and learn and keep an open mind, and amass opinions and convictions and then act on them. Remember that the Bible tells us to say our prayers, but then God expects you to do good deeds.

When you are troubled or angry, talk to your father. Talk to your uncle. Ask me what my father would have said to you. There is a legion of Black men in your life who have faced what you will be facing, and who love you with all their hearts and souls. And they will have advice and wisdom and humor and empathy to share. They will give you a map through the hardships.

But talk to me, too, Zik. Because I will tell you that there are so many ways to be a young Black boy, and so many ways to grow into a strong and loving Black man. You are limitless in your identity. There is no ceiling to who you could become.

And I will also give you Ta-Nehisi's book to read, and I know it will make you feel braver because it will make you feel understood. The written word is something we can return to, and depend on, over and over again.

BOOKS HAVE ALREADY GIVEN US SO MANY GIFTS, ZIK. THEY are what sustains our little family in both philosophical and material ways. They are my passion and my career. And they have allowed me, and now you, to meet and interact with so many incredible people, including our first Black president, Barack Obama.

In 2008, I was twenty-six years old, when President Obama had just been elected, and the world felt like it had changed overnight.

On the day of the inauguration, I hoped to get down to the Mall to see the president be sworn in, but once I started to head down that way, it became clear that the traffic was so terrible there was no way I would get through.

Disappointed, I settled on having brunch with my friend at the Creamery Café, a little restaurant that was directly across from my office, where I knew they would be broadcasting the inaugural festivities. While we were there, I met a reporter from *Newsweek* named Ellis Cose, and we talked for about thirty minutes while we ate our pancakes and watched the inauguration on television.

"Do you mind if I quote you in my article?" he asked. I said I didn't mind at all.

"I spent part of the day in the U Street corridor," he wrote, "an area pretty much destroyed in 1968 by riots following the murder of Martin Luther King Jr. U street is now a bustling commercial strip with trendy eateries, such as Creme Cafe and Lounge, where Glory Edim, a 26-year-old marketing coordinator, dabbed away tears as she watched Obama's speech. 'I never thought this would happen,' said Edim, the daughter of Nigerian immigrants. 'It allows me to believe that whatever I want to achieve in this world, I can.'"

I said that and I meant that, Zik. And it was published in *Newsweek* on February 2, 2009.

And then, thirteen years later, after I started the Well-Read Black Girl Book Club, and just after you were born, I was given the honor of interviewing President Obama myself. His time being president was over, but he had written a book, *A Promised Land*, and he wanted to tell me and the other people in the club all about it. And before I did the interview, which was on Zoom because we were still in the middle of the pandemic, we had the rare opportunity to say hello President Obama, I was holding you in my lap and your father and your grandma—your father's mother— excitedly said hello too.

We were all so excited. I dressed you in a onesie with a

picture of Frederick Douglass on the front, and I thought so hard about what I wanted to say. And when it was time, I held you and I also held President Obama's book, and you tried to chew on the book, and then you dropped the book on the floor and started to fuss, but the president was so kind. When I introduced you to him, he said, "Zikomo! That's a strong name! Like Barack!"

Books gave us that moment, Zik. You might not remember it, but you'll always have the time you met our first Black president, and that was because of a book.

ZIKOMO MEANS *THANK YOU* IN YOUR FATHER'S LANGUAGE, Chichewa. Your nickname, Zik, is an ode to Nnamdi Azikiwe who was the first president of independent Nigeria. A revolutionary leader my father greatly admired. He was fondly called Zik and was a central figure in Nigeria's movement from colonialism to independence. You have a world of meaning in your name, my son. So many stories and aspirations, so much gratitude.

THERE ARE MATERIAL THINGS I WANT YOU TO HAVE, BUT there are other, more essential things, too. Books that you can hold in your hand are important, but words are important, too. Not just the words you read in those books, which are very valuable indeed, but the words we speak and think. The words we choose to name something. The words we use when we are talking to the people we love, and the people we need to stand up against (and sometimes those might be the same people). You're learning to speak right now, and it gives me a rush of pleasure every time you add a new word to your vocabulary. I want to teach you all the words for the emotions, not just happy and sad and mad, but the nuanced range. I want you to know the words for disappointment, frustration, anxiety, amazement, regret, longing, and all the multiple shades of joy. I want you to be able to feel something and name it clearly, use your words as tools, because if you can do that, you can let people into the subtleties of your heart, and your emotional world will be infinite.

AFTER YOU WERE BORN, MY SIBLINGS COULDN'T COME TO visit because of the Covid pandemic. So every morning I would show you a little picture I had of me and Maurice and Tunde. We are so young in that photo—I am in high school, Maurice is in middle school, and Tunde is just a little kid—but it makes me so happy to look at it. It's such a loving picture. And I always imagine that there is a place for you in that photo, that we could easily put your sweet, brown, smiling face right next to ours.

"Family," I would singsong to you every morning, pointing at the picture. "Maurice. Tunde."

And you would smile and maybe reach for the photo, or sometimes you would push it away in favor of a toy or something shinier. But I think you knew how important they were going to be to you, because one of your very first words was *uncle*.

And now we're all together on the East Coast again, and every time you see my brothers you shout "Uncle!" and smile and laugh and give them high fives, and Maurice speaks to you in Spanish so you will learn another language, and Tunde indulges your current obsession with cars and trucks because he is an engineer. And I think you already know they will always be there for you. Whatever you need, Maurice and Tunde are going to be there to guide you through.

IF WE ARE TALKING ABOUT WORDS, WE ARE ALSO NECESsarily talking about truth, which is something else I will teach you to value. Truth is paramount, Zikomo. Truth makes things real. Living your life swamped with lies or insisting that silence makes you strong can only lead to shame and regret. It places you at a distance from your heart and the hearts of the people you love. And I know that sometimes it can be scary to tell the truth. You might think it will get you into trouble, or give someone the opportunity to hurt you. But I think you will find that keeping secrets or telling lies will always result in more pain than simply expressing what really happened and how you truly feel about it.

Don't worry about making mistakes. Don't be scared of failure. You can't learn if you don't fail. Don't ever think you have to perform perfection or be any one certain kind of way in order to be loved. Be yourself, whatever that looks like, and you will be able to trust that the people who matter in your life will love you for exactly who you are.

Having that clarity of self, knowing who you are at your

core, is one of the biggest things I wish for you. It took me a long time to be able to see myself clearly. Sometimes I still think I'm playing catch-up. I spent a long time trying to be someone that I thought other people wanted me to be, and that is time I can't get back. Don't waste your time like that, Zik. Don't be afraid to know yourself and then shine that self-knowledge upon the world.

I LOVE THIS QUOTE BY BENJAMIN FRANKLIN THAT YOUR uncle Maurice and I joke about all the time. We call it "the plans quote": "If you fail to plan, you're planning to fail."

Spontaneity is good. Doing things spur of the moment can be so much fun. So when I talk about planning, I am not talking about being rigid or inflexible, but I need you to know that it is wise to think ahead. It's important to consider as many outcomes as possible and think about how you might react to them. Right now, I am in the season of my life where I treasure solid ground to stand on and a plan to help me strive forward. Planning allows you to manifest things, and then it puts you to work. And work can be one of the great joys of your life.

We had originally planned that you would be born in New York, but the dangers of the pandemic meant that the hospitals in New York weren't even letting fathers in to see their children being born. So, when I was thirty-two weeks pregnant with you (and that is very, very pregnant), your father and I moved to California. It was not our original plan, of course, but plans change, and that is okay.

We had a birth plan, too, but that had to be adjusted

when you refused to come out. The nurse said you were stuck on my left side, just curled up into a little ball, snoozing away, perfectly comfortable, and you didn't think it was necessary to wake up and start the work of coming into this world. So I had a C-section, which was not what I had originally hoped for but had been within our plans if it proved necessary. And it was necessary to make sure that you and I would both be healthy and safe.

So you were born in California, with your father there in the room to meet you, and we played the Bill Withers song "Lovely Day" as you finally entered this world.

And then the Covid rules meant that your father had to go home right after you were born, so for that first night it was just you and me, my baby. And you were so good, so quiet, you hardly cried at all. But I didn't sleep. I didn't want to. I spent the night feeding you and holding you and just looking at you. I couldn't believe you were there. I couldn't believe you were mine. You were the world's greatest mystery and the thing I knew best, all wrapped up into one tiny person. You were the most wonderful thing I had ever been allowed to have.

WHEN WE CAME HOME FROM THE HOSPITAL, MY MOTHER was there waiting to take care of us. And as soon as I saw her, I collapsed into her arms, still holding you. I cried and you cried, and I was just so happy and relieved that my mother was there, ready to show me the way.

For two months she stayed with us, and she cooked and

made sure that I ate so that you could eat. She cleaned so that our house could be sweet for us to live in. She held you so I could sleep. She supported me while I figured out what all the sounds and different cries you made meant. She sang to you and chattered at us both all day long. Her big laugh filled our house. She made me feel like things would be okay.

I was your mother, and I was caring for you, but she was my mother, and she was caring for me.

It's funny to think about it now, but when we first came home, I was very scared of bathing you. I don't know why, except that you were so tiny and fragile, and I was afraid of somehow doing it wrong and hurting you. But your grandma Henrietta said, "This is something you need to know. This is how you give him a bath." And I was still so scared, I didn't even want to watch her! Isn't that silly? But she touched my arm and she looked at me, and she said, "Glory, you have to watch this. You have to learn. For Zik."

And so I did, and now bath time is our favorite thing.

AND PLEASE LISTEN, ZIKOMO, IT WAS NEVER IN THE PLAN for your father and I not to stay together. One of the hardest things I ever had to do was change that plan. But it will always, always, be in the plan for both of us to love you, and care for you, and listen to you, and make you the center of our worlds.

I promise you, that plan will never be altered.

———

BEFORE ANY OF US ARE BORN, THERE ARE ANCESTORS UPON ancestors thinking and creating and dreaming about us. I know that my father, your grandfather, wanted a grandson. He was longing to see you be born, Zikomo. And it makes me feel tender and sad that he couldn't be there for that. But you have my eyes, and I have my father's eyes, so when I look at you, the miracle is that we are all here, together, after all.

YOU WERE A DREAM FOR MY MOTHER, YOUR GRANDmother, as well. You were a dream that came to fruition. Our family is small, and you made it bigger. You are an extension of us, another child born of our lineage, the Edims. Your father gave you your first name, but I gave you your second, so you carry that piece of us as well. You are half of your father, but half of me, too, and so there will never be a time when you are not an Edim.

THESE DAYS, THE BOOK YOU LOVE MOST IS CALLED *GOOD Night, Wiggly Toes* by Roda Ahmed and Leandra Rose. It's about a little girl who isn't ready to go to sleep, so her mommy helps her find a way to relax and let go. We read it almost every night, naming all the parts of your body that need to stop working so hard and rest so that you can sleep. And as I read to you, you yawn and stretch and snuggle up against me, and you let the words work their magic and lead you into your dreams.

———

BOOKS MADE ME WHO I AM, ZIK. THEY GAVE ME WISDOM and laughter, beauty and truth. Books challenged me and comforted me; they made me stretch and grow. Books showed me how to dream and plan. They made me cry in big, gasping, ugly sobs. Books made me furious. Sometimes they put me to sleep. Books made me nostalgic and gave me great hope for the future. They gave me a mirror to look into. A voice to my pain. They showed me a path. They lifted me to the stars. They let me escape to a new world when the world I was living in was barely survivable.

I was saved by books, my little son.

Books and words are what I have to offer you. They are your inheritance. They are your legacy. They are the truest manifestation of my love.

And so I hope that you're reading this letter—I hope you're reading these words—and that this book will be one of many books that will leave an impression on your heart and soul.

Get to reading, Zikomo!

Love always,
Mommy

AFTERWORD

When I look back, I am so impressed again with the life-giving power of literature. If I were a young person today, trying to gain a sense of myself in the world, I would do that again by reading, just as I did when I was young.

—MAYA ANGELOU

Reading is a practice that saves my life every day. Writing these pages has been an exercise in vulnerability, introspection, and, ultimately, healing. It has been a privilege to share my story, to open windows into the rooms of my past, and to invite you, dear reader, into the most intimate corners of my life. I've had an opportunity to reread old books and childhood diaries, revisit forgotten hardships and joyful memories. But Audre Lorde once wrote, "Our feelings are our most genuine paths to knowledge," and I wholeheartedly agree. My feelings have guided me through every step of this journey. Giving birth to my son and subsequently writing this memoir somehow increased my sense of amazement with the world. I became less cynical and started noticing all the things I had missed before—the space between hearing and listening, looking and seeing. I no longer want to read my way through triumphs and tribulations. I want to be present. I am eager to experience a creative, well-lived life, to find meaning in everyday meditations and language.

In *The Color Purple*, Alice Walker writes, "I think us here to wonder, myself. To wonder. To ask. And that in wondering bout the big things and asking bout the big things, you learn about the little ones, almost by accident. But you never know nothing more about the big things than you start out with. The more I wonder, the more I love." She captures the profound connections between personal transformation, curiosity, and empathy. Walker understood the value of engaging deeply with the world. They all did—Toni Morrison, Audre Lorde, Lucille Clifton, Nikki Giovanni, Toni Cade Bambara, the list goes on and on. The more time we devote to wonder, the more our capacity for love expands. The more I wonder, the more I love. To be well-read is a transformative way of being in and with the world. It hinges on curiosity and the desire for freedom, whether that looks like reading a book or holding my child's hand. To be a generous neighbor, to plant a garden, to share a meal, to help my community flourish, to empower readers everywhere to stand together in the fight against inequality and censorship. To wonder. To love. To fight for goodness and mercy. To be, in a word, alive.

As I close this chapter of my life, I do so with a heart full of immense gratitude. I hope that my story has touched you in some way and that you carry forward the reflections it has inspired. May we all continue to share our stories, to listen with genuine curiosity, and to find strength in our collective humanity. Thank you for being a part of this journey.

ACKNOWLEDGMENTS

I have so many people to thank for helping to bring this memoir to fruition.

First and foremost, I am so thankful to have the support of my beloved family. To my parents, who instilled in me the values of resilience and curiosity. To my siblings, for their endless encouragement and for reminding me of the importance of laughter and love. To my son, whose joyful presence in my life has been a constant source of strength.

This book would not exist without my editor Emily Hartley. Thank you for believing in my vision and guiding me through those early stages. You were ever-present and always encouraging throughout this process.

Thank you to my incredible literary agent, Emma Parry. I am so grateful for your thoughtfulness and care. Your guidance has been instrumental to my literary journey.

My heartfelt thanks to Maia Rossini, for many hours of

collaboration, brainstorming, and excavating memories. Your moral support and deep belief in this project were a lifeline.

To the teachers, librarians, and mentors who have guided me along the way, thank you for your wisdom, and for igniting my passion for storytelling. Mr. Burns, your lessons and kindness have stayed with me and continue to inspire me.

At Ballantine, a wonderful group of professionals has seen the manuscript through to book form: Sara Weiss, Sydney Collins, Allison Schuster, Jordan Hill Forney, Emily Isayeff, Rachel Ake, and many more. Thank you for your talent and dedication. I am so grateful for your hard work on this book!

I am immensely grateful to my friends, who have been my sounding boards, my critics, and my biggest supporters. Your honest feedback, late-night conversations, and unwavering faith in my abilities have been invaluable. Thank you for sharing loving notes of encouragement throughout the making of this book. Thank you to Ida, Selma, and Petrushka for keeping me honest and helping me fact-check my high school memories. To the DC-area ladies—Bsrat, Yelena, Chelsea, and Lula—for always keeping me grounded and making me laugh. To my college roommate, Gimari Ladd-Jones, who lovingly reminds me how far I've come since HU. The Brooklyn to Los Angeles book club members turned lifelong friends—Jehan, Latoya, Mavis, and Tameka—our sisterhood is deeply appreciated.

Finally, I owe a debt of gratitude to all the supporters of the Well-Read Black Girl community. This memoir is a testament to the power of community, love, and perseverance. I hope that my story resonates with you and perhaps even inspires you to reflect on your own.

To everyone named in this book, thank you for inspiring and supporting me. Thank you for allowing me to share a part of your lives in these pages. Excited to close this chapter and begin anew. Onward!

ABOUT THE AUTHOR

GLORY EDIM is an author, entrepreneur, and literary advocate for diverse writers in publishing. In 2015, she founded Well-Read Black Girl (WRBG), an online platform and book club dedicated to celebrating the works of Black women writers. Under Glory's leadership, WRBG has grown into a non-profit organization which produces the Well-Read Black Girl literary festival. Her efforts to elevate underrepresented voices have garnered widespread recognition and praise, earning her accolades such as the 2017 Innovator's Award from the *Los Angeles Times* and the Madam C.J. Walker Award from the Hurston/Wright Foundation. As an author herself, Glory has contributed to the literary landscape with her best-selling anthologies *Well-Read Black Girl: Finding Our Stories, Discovering Ourselves,* and *On Girlhood: 15 Stories from the Well-Read Black Girl Library.*

Through advocacy and storytelling, Glory continues to curate a unique space where Black writers are centered, celebrated, and given the recognition they deserve in the publishing industry. She remains steadfast in her mission to create a more inclusive and equitable world where every voice is heard and valued.

gloryedim.com
wellreadblackgirl.org